Looking East

The Story of Gold

By Xiang Zhonghua

Foreign Languages Press

First Edition 2006

ISBN 7-119-04521-0
© Foreign Languages Press, Beijing, China, 2006
Published by Foreign Languages Press
24 Baiwanzhuang Road, Beijing 100037, China
Website:http://www.flp.com.cn
Email Address://Info@flp.com.cn
Sales@flp.com.cn
Distributed by China International Book Trading Corporation
35 Chegongzhuang Xilu, Beijing 100044, China
P.O. Box 399, Beijing, China
Printed in the People's Republic of China

Contents

Preface *I*

Chapter 1 **Where Does Gold Come From?** *001*
China, One of the Earliest Countries Mining Gold *002*
Sources of Gold in Ancient China *006*
Panning for Gold *010*

Chapter 2 **Gold Jewelry in the Shang and Zhou Dynasties** *011*
Shang Dynasty Gold Utensils and Vessels *012*
Gold Vessels and Utensils Unearthed at Sanxingdui and Jinsha *015*
Gold Vessels of the Western Zhou Dynasty *020*

Contents

Chapter 3   Spring and Autumn and Warring States Periods—The Early Years of Gold Luxury Goods   *023*

Gold Objects Found in China's Central Plains   *024*

Gold Cup from Tomb of Marquis Yi of Zeng   *027*

Gold-handled Swords and Belt Hooks Unearthed at Yimen Village   *029*

Xiongnu Gold Crown   *032*

Chapter 4   Gold Ware in Qin and Han Dynasties, and Its Magical Significance   *035*

Gold Ware of the Qin Dynasty   *036*

Han Dynasty Jade Burial Suit Sewn with Fine Gold Threads   *038*

Gold Seals and the Seal Engraving Art of the Han Dynasty   *040*

Han Dynasty Gold Coins   *044*

Funeral Objects from Officials' Tombs   *046*

Chapter 5 Objects with Western Characteristics from the Wei and Jin and Southern and Northern Dynasties Periods 053

Gold Collections of the Aristocracy 054
Utensils and Vessels with a Foreign Flavor 058
The Coming of Buddhism 062

Chapter 6 Tang Dynasty, the Heyday of Gold Artistry 065

Property of the Rich and Powerful 066
Tea and Buddhism 069
Gold Objects Presented to the Tang Emperors 073
The Aesthetics of Gold 075
Decorative Patterns 077
Cream of the Prosperous Tang Dynasty 079
Emergence of the South 081

Contents

Chapter 7 **Gold Wares in the Song and Liao Dynasties** *083*

Slim, Changeable and Antique in Form *084*
Simple and Poetic Decorative Patterns *086*
Gold for Decorative, Daily-life and Buddhist Use *091*
Creative Craftsmanship *093*
Gold Ware of the Liao Dynasty *094*
Golden-winged Bird from the Kingdom of Dali *100*

Chapter 8 **Gold Jewelry from the Yuan and Ming Dynasties, Heyday of Veteran Craftsmen** *101*

Rise of Handicraft Workshops *102*
Unique Products *104*
Luxury Jewelry *106*
Vessels with Gold and Jade Inlay *110*

Chapter 9   Flying Dragons and the Qing Dynasty   113

Imperial Ceremonial Objects   114

Imperial Treasures   120

Imperial Tableware   123

Imperial Buddhist Ceremonial Objects   124

Gold Seals of the Qing Dynasty   126

Gold and China's National Ethics   128

Preface

The history of gold is as ancient as that of mankind. It ignited the passions of human beings as long ago as 12,000 years, when the eternal search for gold, whether as wealth or ornament, started. Gold has long been a symbol of wealth from the days of the ancient empires to the present, although gold is neither the hardest, most durable or rarest metal. Through its approach to gold, we can sense the nature of a culture. The history of gold reveals its qualities, its interaction with the various peoples of the world, its relations with the times, its unmatchable beauty, and its rich and complicated characteristics.

Gold affects human life deeply as an icon. From the very start, the quality of people's life or a culture seems to have been closely linked with the glamour of gold. It could be a symbol of male power, as is the gold scepter unearthed at Sanxingdui (the site of a kingdom which flourished on the Chengdu Plain in the 17th century BC), and the gold seals and monarchs' crowns from China's feudal times. Females also valued gold highly for making ornaments to enhance their beauty.

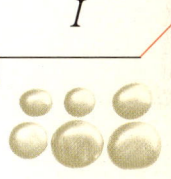

The Story of Gold

Out of this passion emerged gold craftsmen and their art. Gold itself is a touchstone of the permanent dialogue between man and Nature, inseparable from the most colorful and glamorous part of a culture. Stories about gold are prominent in the myths and legends of all peoples. While the owners of gold vessels inevitably pass away, gold continues through the ages, aloof from the world's changes. With its sublime power of demanding worship and as a substance imbued with man's highest artistic impulses, gold has obtained immortality.

From the ancient gold objects unearthed so far, it can be concluded that items made of gold were available as early as the Shang Dynasty (17th-11th centuries BC). But, gilt coating is found on bronze ware from the earlier Erlitou site in Yanshi, Henan Province. Some scholars think that this site belongs to what is thought to have been the Xia Dynasty (ca. 2071-1600 BC), which is referred to in ancient records, but for which there is no archeological evidence, while some hold that the Erlitou culture marks the transition from the Xia Dynasty to the Shang Dynasty. Chinese gold craftsmanship has come down to us in a continuous tradition for thousands of years as a unique artistic genre, with varieties of rare and valuable products.

It is estimated that gold constitutes a mere billionth of the contents of the earth's crust, and it is likely that the earliest findings of it were specks or tiny lumps come upon by chance in stream beds. The technique of pan-washing river sand to obtain gold then emerged.

A rare metal, gold warms people with its charming shine and it is naturally linked with such fine expressions as nobility, hope and eternity. Gold products symbolize man's long and continuous history. And the wisdom, cultural genetic code, artistic sensibilities and technological skill it displays represent the most beautiful and timeless part of human history.

Panning for gold has been practiced throughout China's history to the present day, representing the arduous and complicated formation of the history of its people. Placer gold is obtained only after the sand is pan-washed again and again, just like a person's growth or the process of the formation of a culture. Traditional Chinese culture has undergone a similar long and arduous process. Ancient gold mines and streams where gold was panned remind us of the wells and flows of history.

The glitter of gold burnishes the whole of human history.

■ Gold cup inlaid with gems, Qing Dynasty

 IV

Chapter 1
Where Does Gold Come From?

Gold does not exist in large ore bodies in Nature, but in small amounts embedded in other materials.

It can be divided into pure gold and alloy gold (or K gold), according to the percentage of gold content. "Pure gold" jewelry actually has a content of more that 99 percent, even up to 99.99 percent. So, it is also called 99 gold or pure gold. K gold jewelry consists of a gold alloy, together with such materials as silver and bronze, and is marked with a letter K.

■ Gold panning site

The Story of Gold

China, One of the Earliest Countries Mining Gold

Concentrated locations of gold exist, and they are mined by the usual extractive methods. Placer gold is washed downstream to a riverbed from deposits.

Experienced gold miners say that even when only 10 g or so of gold can be extracted from a ton of mineral ore, or a few tenths of a g of gold can be extracted from a cubic meter of sands, it is still worth exploiting. Mineral ores vary in size and depth, and it could be a few years or dozens of years at the most before the deposit is exhausted.

China was one of the first places in the world to extract and use gold. According to the *Guanzi*, a book compiled by Liu Xiang during the Han Dynasty (206 BC-25 AD), the area now roughly comprising Hubei and Hunan provinces in southern China was famous for gold production along the Ruhe and Hanshui rivers. This region was ruled by the

■ Ancient gold seals of China

■ A laced gold box cover with dragon design for a jade container, Ming Dynasty, found in the Ding Mausoleum, Beijing

State of Chu, which flourished during the Warring States Period (475-221 BC) of the Zhou Dynasty (11th century-256 BC). In its heyday, Chu covered an area of some one million sq km and had a population of one quarter of the whole of that of China.

It was in the State of Chu too that gold currency (in bullions) was first issued in China. Usually pressed with two characters *ying yuan* or *chen yuan* (both *ying* and *chen*

The Story of Gold

Gold bracelets, Ming Dynasty

were place names, and the character *yuan* is thought to be an ancient weight unit.) As proved by archeological discoveries, the currency's wide circulation covered such places as Hefei, Lujiang, Guangde, Liu'an, Funan, Shouxian, Chaoxian and Linquan in Anhui Province, Xi'an and Xianyang in Shaanxi Province, Nanjing, Jiangyin, Peixian, Danyang and Jiangning of Jiangsu Province. *Ying yuan* gold bullions usually weighed 280 g with 10-20 marks and the biggest one found so far weighs 610 g and has 54 marks.

Before the Spring and Autumn Period (722-481 BC), the Chinese character *jin*, meaning "gold," meant not only gold, but also silver and, more often, bronze. The ancient book *Records of the Historian* tells us: "Long ago, gold had three categories—yellow, white and red." These colors can be identified as indicating gold, silver and bronze, respectively. The character *jin* referred solely to gold only from the Warring States Period (475-221 BC).

There is a famous Chinese story called "Winning a smile with 1,000 *liang* of gold." (A traditional Chinese unit of weight, one *liang* is equivalent to 31.25 g). King You of the Zhou Dynasty, upset by his favorite concubine's gloomy countenance, racked his brains for some way to make her smile. A man named Guo Shifu then suggested to the king that he send a fake war alarm, calling for help from his vassal princes. The concubine burst into a smile when she saw troops hastening to the capital on a fool's errand. Guo was rewarded with 1,000 *liang* of gold for his idea, hence the title of the story.

Historical records make it clear that the mining of gold, as well as of jade, tin and marble, was a state monopoly almost from the start, showing that the value of these rare minerals was recognized at a very early date.

■ Gold bubbles, Spring and Autumn Period, found at Fengxiang, Shaanxi Province

The Story of Gold

Sources of Gold in Ancient China

During the Qin (221-206 BC) and Western Han (206 BC-8 AD) dynasties, gold production developed rapidly. According to the *Records of the Historian*, the state treasury had more than 400,000 *jin* (a *jin* is a traditional Chinese unit of weight, equivalent to 0.5 kg). During the Western Han Dynasty, gold bars and hoof-shaped round bucks circulated as currency. Alchemists believed that gold had medicinal properties, and one alchemist, Li Shaojun, who lived during the reign of Han Dynasty Emperor Wu (156-87 BC), claimed that longevity could be realized through the use of gold or silver vessels. This was a strong

■ Long-stemmed gold cup with engraved flower design, Yuan Dynasty, found in Baotou, Inner Mongolia Autonomous Region

■ Ying yuan, gold coin of the State of Chu, Warring States Period.

incentive for the production and use of gold and silver utensils.

Emperor Wu was one of the first rulers of China to require his vassals to present gold as tribute to him. This gold was used to make sacrificial vessels for ancestor worship. Failure to present gold of sufficient purity could result in the demotion of a noble. For instance, Emperor Wu used this pretext to remove the titles of nobility of more than 100 people. In Western Han times, gold production was centered along the Jinsha River, on the upper reaches of the Yangtze River. Other important areas of gold production were the Ruhe and Hanshui river valleys, Lingyang in present-day Anhui Province, Poyang in present-day Jiangxi Province and Nanshan in the present-day Xinjiang Uygur Autonomous Region.

The areas of today's Sichuan and Yunnan provinces were added to the list during the Eastern Han Dynasty (25-220); panning for gold in Mianyang and Guangyuan in Sichuan is still practiced at the present day.

From the Tang Dynasty (618-907) to the Qing Dynasty (1644-1911), placer gold production and gold mining spread nationwide. The main production areas were in what

007
Where Does Gold Come From?

The Story of Gold

■ Chen yuan, another kind of gold coin of the State of Chu, Warring States Period

are now the provinces of Sichuan, Yunnan, Hunan, Shandong, Xinjiang, Hubei, Guizhou, Shaanxi and Gansu, and the Guangxi Zhuang Autonomous Region.

During the Tang Dynasty, Shanglin County in Guangxi and Changde in Hunan were important gold mining centers. In the Song Dynasty (960-1279), river placer gold production was mainly carried on in southern China in such places as the Youjiang River valley in Guangxi, Yichang in Hubei Province, and Liling, Changde and Jingxian in Hunan Province. Laizhou and Dengzhou in Shandong Province were two of the most important gold-production areas in the Yuan (1271-1368) and Ming (1368-1644) dynasties.

New gold deposits were found in the Yuan Dynasty, in such areas as Yidu and Qixia in Shandong Province, Dali, Chuxiong, Lijiang, Yuanjiang, Zhaotong and Baoshan in Yunnan Province, Yuezhou, Yuanzhou, Jingzhou, Chenzhou, Tanzhou and Baoqing in Hunan Province, Jiangling and Xiangyang in Hubei Province, and Hezhou in Xinjiang. Traditional gold production developed further in Kaiyuan in Jilin Province, and Daning, Longshan and

Shuangcheng in Liaoning Province.

During the Ming Dynasty, placer gold production was concentrated in such areas as Lijiang in Yunnan Province, and Guangyuan, Tongchuan, Zhaohua, Hexian and Bazhou in Sichuan Province. In the Qing Dynasty, gold mines flourished in Sichuan, Yunnan, Shaanxi, Gansu and Hunan provinces, with the output of the Dunhuang area of Gansu Province ranking first in the country. Gold mining continued to develop in the Qing Dynasty, and in 1888 China's nationwide production was ranked fifth in the world, with an output of 13.5 tons, which was seven percent of the global total.

In modern China, gold production remains a state monopoly under the China Gold Co. Ltd., mainly because the cost of modern methods of extraction is beyond private capacity. However, private placer gold production exists in a few traditional areas. The main gold-production sites in today's China are Lesser Hinggan Mountains in Heilongjiang Province, and Zhaoyuan and Yantai in Shandong Province.

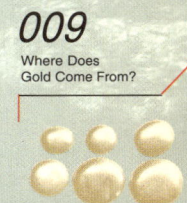

009
Where Does Gold Come From?

■ Gold arm rings, Han Dynasty, found in Kangzhuang Town, Yanqing District, Beijing

Panning for Gold

The earliest and simplest method of collecting gold was panning. This involves swirling river sand in a pan, until the gold particles, which are heavier than the sand, settle in the bottom of the pan. The water and sand are then poured out.

During the Song Dynasty placer mining, as panning is also called, was done on a bigger scale, when primitive wooden sluices were installed on gold-bearing streams and rivers.

The renowned philosopher Wang Yangming (1472-1528) used an analogy based on gold to describe the ideal Confucian personality: Gold can vary in weight from one jin (a traditional Chinese unit of weight, equivalent to half a kg) to 10,000 *jin*, or one *liang* to 10,000 *liang*, but the weight has little connection with the purity or value of the gold. Confucianists put more emphasis on the importance of purity or quality than on quantity.

■ Gold-plated belt, Northern Song Dynasty, found on Shangxiachuan Island, Guangdong Province

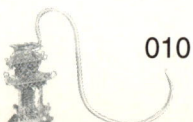

Chapter 2
Gold Jewelry in the Shang and Zhou Dynasties

So far, no pieces of gold or gold vessels have been found at any sites of cultural remains dating from before the Shang Dynasty (1600-1046 BC), only gold in the simple form of decorative foil, leaves or thin slices. Small gold-decorated vessels have been found dating from both the Shang and Zhou (1046-256 BC) dynasties.

Gold was outranked in importance by copper and bronze during the latter two dynasties, bronze vessels being used for religious and state ceremonies. Among China's earliest inscriptions on bones and tortoise shells, dating from the Shang Dynasty, are characters for "gold" in the shape of open shells. Now, it is known that cowrie shells were in use as currency at that time, and the shape of the character for "gold" hence suggests that the precious metal had a value as currency.

■ Sun-shaped gold foil ornament with bird design, Shang Dynasty, found in Jinsha Village, Chengdu, Sichuan Province

Shang Dynasty Gold Utensils and Vessels

Flattened pieces of gold carrying patterns commonly seen on Shang Dynasty bronzewares have been found in the ruins of the Shang cities of Anyang and Zhengzhou, in Henan Province. Gold foil dating from the same period shows that the art of beating gold was known at that time, and gold threads found in a Shang Dynasty tomb in Linzheyu, Shanxi Province, are more proof of the craftsmen's expertise. Clouds and thunder patterns are found carved on a gold decoration on the surface of the re-

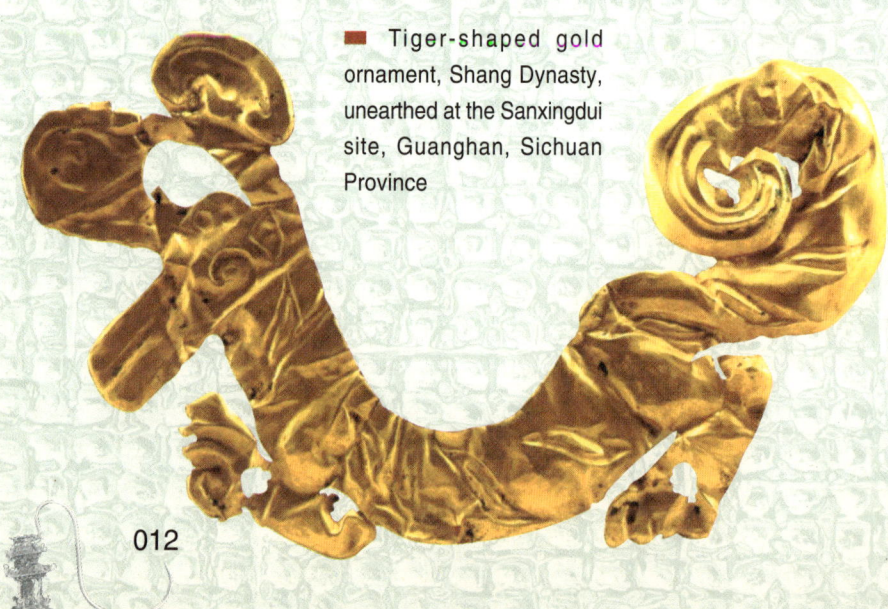

■ Tiger-shaped gold ornament, Shang Dynasty, unearthed at the Sanxingdui site, Guanghan, Sichuan Province

■ Gold mask, Shang Dynasty, unearthed at the Sanxingdui site

mains of a lacquer case excavated at a Shang Dynasty site in Taixi Village, Hebei Province, showing a high degree of workmanship. In some Shang tombs, bronze jewelry has been unearthed together with gold decorations, with similar shapes and structures. The vivid northwestern style of these decorations is evidence that that area was rich in gold in ancient times.

The most famous gold articles from the Shang Dynasty were found in two locations—a set of jewelry from a tomb at Liujiahe, Pinggu County, Beijing, and a gilded scepter and gilded bronze sculptures of human heads unearthed at Sanxingdui, in Sichuan Province, in addition to several pieces of gold jewelry excavated at the Jinsha site in Chengdu, Sichuan Province.

Gold objects including earrings, bracelets, hairpins and scraps of gold foil were found in a Shang Dynasty tomb in 1977 at Liujiahe, Beijing. These objects have a gold content of above 85 percent, together with small amounts of silver and copper. The gold hairpin was mold-cast, and the earrings and the bracelets were hammered out. The objects are simple and plain in style, and don't have any pat-

The Story of Gold

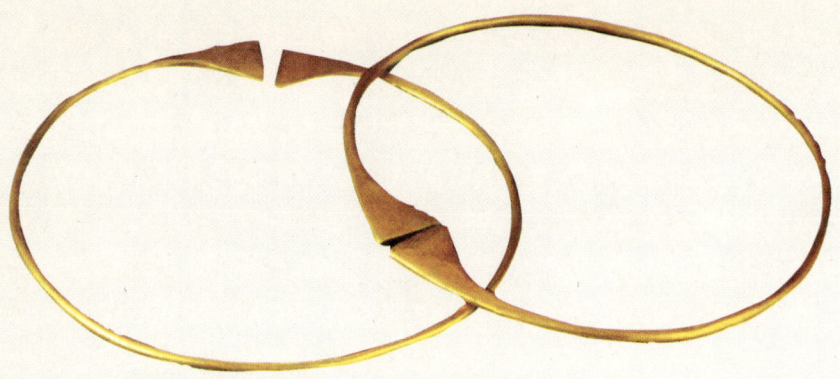

■ Gold armlets, Shang Dynasty, found in the Liujiahe Tomb

terns or decorations on them. They constitute the earliest set of gold jewelry unearthed so far in China.

The gold hairpin is 27.7 cm long, with a width of 2.9 cm at the head and 0.9 cm at the tail end. It weighs 108.7 g. With an obtuse triangular cross-section, it has a 0.4-cm-long tendon structure at the base, which hints that there might be some decorations around that part.

The gold earrings are 3.4 cm long, and weigh 6.8 g. Fan-shaped at the lower part, they have an awl-shaped upper end.

The two gold bracelets weigh 79.8 g and 93.7 g, respectively. They were made using gold bars 0.3 cm in diameter and bent in a circle, with the connecting ends hammered flat to fan-shaped. Despite their age of more than 3,000 years, they still shine brightly.

Gold Vessels and Utensils Unearthed at Sanxingdui and Jinsha

At roughly the same time as the Central Plains Cul-ture flourished during the Shang Dynasty, there was another robust culture in the Sichuan Basin in southwest China. The Sanxingdui Culture, named after the village where the first relics of it were found, had its own distinct treatment of gold vessels, pottery and bronze human figures.

Located south of the Yazi (Duck) River, the Sanxingdui site is located 10 km west of Guanghan, Sichuan Province, with the Muma River flowing through the site. The No. 1 and No. 2 sacrificial pits, discovered in 1986, are located to the southeast of the Muma River. Unearthed here were

■ Gold hair-pin, Shang Dynasty, found in the Liujiahe Tomb, Pinggu County, Beijing

The Story of Gold

a larger number of relics made of gold, bronze, jade, stone and pottery, including sacred trees, human images, altars, birds and some mysterious figures. Among the over 100 gold pieces are a scepter, male face masks, leaves and ornaments shaped like tigers or fish, or round in form. This makes Sanxingdui a Shang Dynasty period site where the most gold relics have been unearthed. The objects' unique and mysterious shapes, the strange location of the Sanxingdui civilization in an isolated basin surrounded by mountains and the culture's mysterious disappearance make the gold vessels all the more intriguing and valuable.

The most impressive items among the relics unearthed at Sanxingdui are a bronze sculpture of a human head and bronze male face masks. Some of the bronze masks have bulging eyes,

■ Gold ear pendants, Shang Dynasty, found in the Liujiahe Tomb

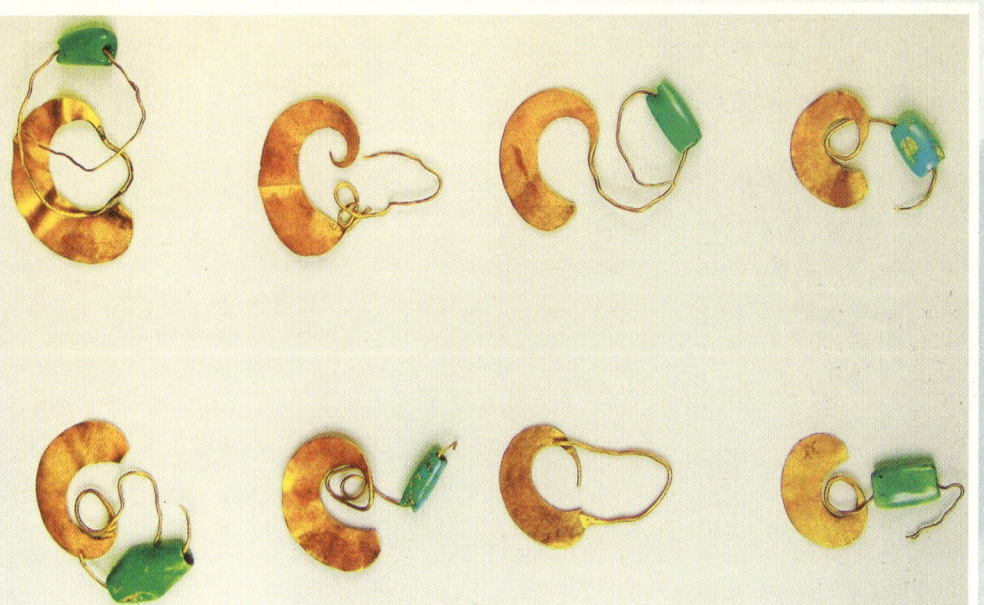

■ Gold earrings, Shang Dynasty, unearthed at Taohua Village, Shanxi Province

which might symbolize Cancong, the first king of the ancient state of Shu. Some images have masks made of hammered gold foil, and are thought to represent shamans called Nuo, who were believed to be capable of driving out evil spirits and warding off disasters by performing ceremonial dances during the Shang and Zhou dynasties.

Also unearthed at Sanxingdui was a scepter, 142 cm long, 2.3 cm in diameter and weighing 500 g. The wooden inner part has rotted away almost completely, but the gold covering is as good as new. The 46-cm-long upper part of the scepter features designs such as a pair of fishes back to back and a pair of birds also back to back. The fishes' heads and birds' necks all have tassel-shaped leafstalk

The Story of Gold

■ Gold belt ornaments, Western Zhou Dynasty, found in a tomb of the State of Guo, Sanmenxia, Henan Province

patterns and symmetrical images of high-crowned human heads with triangular ear ornaments. Animal-patterned decorations are common on gold, silver and bronze vessels of the Shang and Zhou dynasties. At that time, it was thought that wizards needed the help of animals to communicate with the gods. The gold scepter was an instrument used in ceremonies for communication between man and the gods. The human head images on the scepter are believed to represent either kings of the ancient State of Shu or the shamans themselves. The realistic style of the patterns is very similar to that seen on bronze vessels used at that time in the Central Plains area.

Another of the relics is a 12-cm-long tiger-shaped ornament in gold foil. The tiger is rearing up as if about to attack. It is accompanied by eye- and leaf-shaped patterns.

Unearthed at the Jinsha site, which is believed to date from the later stage of Sanxingdui Culture, were more than 40 gold vessels, which show close links in shape, patterns and style with those unearthed at Sanxingdui. One bears a gold decoration depicting four birds flying around the sun, which is as vividly styled as a modern paper-cut.

The Jinsha site probably arose as the Sanxingdui Culture declined. It may be the site of the capital city of Shu during the Western Zhou Dynasty. The gorgeous style of the gold, bronze, jade, pottery and ivory relics found there shows that there was another unique and shining regional civilization independent of the culture of the Central Plains area. The impressive number of gold relics unearthed at this site in Sichuan Province is in stark contrast to the small number found at Shang Dynasty sites.

019
Gold Jewelry in the
Shang and Zhou Dynasties

The Story of Gold

Gold Vessels of the Western Zhou Dynasty

Only 12 gold ornaments, with a total weight of 433 g, dating from the Western Zhou period (1046-771 BC) have been unearthed so far. They were found in a tomb of the State of Guo, located in Sanmenxia City, Henan Province. Seven of these mold-cast objects are round, one is rectangular, three bear animal patterns and one is triangular with animal patterns. These objects were found around the waist of the tomb's occupant, and are thus believed to be belt ornaments.

A painted wooden wine vessel called a *gu* was found in a State of Yan (Warring States Period) tomb in the suburbs of Beijing. There are three strips of gold around the vessel, with turquoise inlays on the two lower strips. This is the earliest relic unearthed so far made with the so-called ground-out gold-inlay technique. This technique requires gold foil to be attached to the object under several lays of paint. When the paint dries out it is carefully ground away to reveal the gold foil pattern underneath.

■ Gold shells, Qijia Culture, found in Datong, Qinghai Province

021
Gold Jewelry in the
Shang and Zhou Dynasties

The Story of Gold

■ Gold wand, Shang Dynasty, unearthed at the Sanxingdui site

Chapter 3
Spring and Autumn and Warring States Periods—The Early Years of Gold Luxury Goods

As the central power of the Zhou monarchs declined, the Spring and Autumn Period came to an end and was succeeded by the Warring States Period. There was a concomitant weakening in the importance of rituals, and in the high regard for sacred bronze vessels. In the anarchy of the Warring States Period, gold and silver became more highly valued than bronze.

The increase in demand spurred increased efforts to produce gold, and vessels and utensils were made which had a high gold content rather than being sparsely decorated with gold foil and strips. It was at this time too that objects made of a gold-iron or gold-copper alloy appeared.

■ Gold cup, Warring States Period, found in the tomb of Marquis Yi of Zeng

The Story of Gold

Gold Objects Found in China's Central Plains

Gold vessels, utensils and ornaments were made for the exclusive use of the aristocracy. Gold became a symbol of wealth and power— as it still is. In the Central Plains area, the center of bronze civilization, gold objects were not manufactured in large numbers during the Spring and Autumn and Warring States periods. But, they tended to be impressively large. The techniques of gold-inlaying and gold-plating developed rapidly.

Relics found in tombs of the late Warring States Period in Yimen Village, Baoji, Shaanxi Province, of the State of Wei in Guwei Village, Huixian County, Henan Province, and in the tomb of King of State of Zhongshan in Pingshan County, Hebei Province, are the most representative of the Central Plains gold vessels in this era. Also notable are gold objects found in a Warring States tomb in Zhongtong Village, Xinle County, Heibei Province, the site of a Spring and Autumn Period State of Qin ancestral temple in Majiazhuang, Fengxiang County, Shaanxi Province, and Tomb No. 126 in Fenshuiling, Changzhi, Shanxi Province.

Among the gold objects from the tomb of King of State

of Zhongshan, excavated in 1977, are a dragon-shaped gold plate with turquoise inlays, a gold cup with a spiral decoration, a belt hook with gold and silver inlays, necklaces, and horse and vehicle trappings. But, the most impressive of these finds are a gold *zun* (wine vessel), a gold-inlaid silver table with dragon-and-phoenix patterns and a gold-and-silver-inlaid table set with a pattern of a tiger killing a deer. Standing 21.3 cm high and weighing 903 g, the gold *zun* could have been one of the biggest gold vessels at that time. The middle part of the vessel has two symmetrical semi-relief figures of dragons, with blue-glazed eyes and silver-inlaid wings and horns. The vessel has a drum-shaped upper part, and an octagonal base with a carved pattern of dragon scales.

The Central Plains, one of the cradles of Chinese civilization, soon eclipsed all other areas of China in prosperity and power. And it was here that the techniques of

025
Spring and Autumn and Warring States Periods—The Early Years of Gold Luxury Goods

■ Gold belt hooks, Warring States Period, found in the tomb of the Marquis Yi of Zeng

The Story of Gold

■ Gold ornament with design of a tiger and wolf fighting, Warring States Period, found in Dongsheng City (Ik Ju League), Inner Mongolia Autonomous Region

decorative gold working was developed to an exquisite degree in the Spring and Autumn and Warring States periods, mainly in the forms of wrapping, inlaying and plating.

The fascination with gold at this time was so strong that there is a story about a certain man of the State of Qi who took gold objects from a shop and walked away without paying for them. Quickly arrested and asked why he had been so foolish as to steal the items with so many people around, he replied: "I saw nobody. All I could see was the gold!"

There is another story from the same period about the famous general Wu Zixu of the State of Chu who sought out a woman who had helped him in adversity. Learning that she had drowned in a river, he threw a bag of gold into the river at the spot where she had drowned as a reward for her kindness.

Gold Cup from Tomb of Marquis Yi of Zeng

The most important gold relics from the Spring and Autumn and Warring States Period are considered to be those found in the tomb of Marquis Yi of the State of Zeng, in Suixian County, Hubei Province. Among them are 950 pieces of gold foil with various impressed patterns, which were probably decorations on the surface of vessels which have long since disintegrated.

Also found in the tomb was a wine cup with a cover, weighing 2,156 g—the heaviest gold object ever found dating from that period. It was mold-cast, the usual technique for manufacturing bronze ware. The cover has a ring-

027
Spring and Autumn and Warring States Periods—The Early Years of Gold Luxury Goods

■ String of gold beads, Spring and Autumn Period, found in Yimen Village

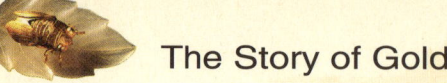

The Story of Gold

■ A gold-inlaid square table with a dragon-and-phoenix design, Warring States Period, found in the tomb of King of Zhongshan, Pingshan County, Hebei Province

shaped handle and two side fastening clips. The cup has S-shaped phoenix claws and two symmetrical ring-shaped ears, with convoluted patterns of *Chi* (hornless dragon), clouds and lightning. The shape and decorative patterns are reminiscent of those of bronze caldrons.

Unearthed at the same time was a drum-shaped gold cup, with a dome cover and fastening clips around the body but no decorative pattern. With a thick wall, the cup weighs 789.9 g, and is believed to have been hammered out.

Gold-handled Swords and Belt Hooks Unearthed at Yimen Village

A total of 104 pure gold, gold-copper and gold-iron alloy vessels were found in 1992 from a tomb in Yimen Village, Shaanxi Province. With a total weight of more than 3,000 g, the finds include strings of beads, belt hooks, buttons, knives, swords and horse and vehicle trappings. Such a large number of precious objects are a rare find for this period.

Among this hoard are two gold-handled iron swords and two gold-decorated knives, one made of iron and the other of copper. The gold sword handles bear convoluted dragon patterns, and were precision-cast with a wax mold, a technique usually used in the manufacturing of bronze

029
Spring and Autumn and Warring States Periods—The Early Years of Gold Luxury Goods

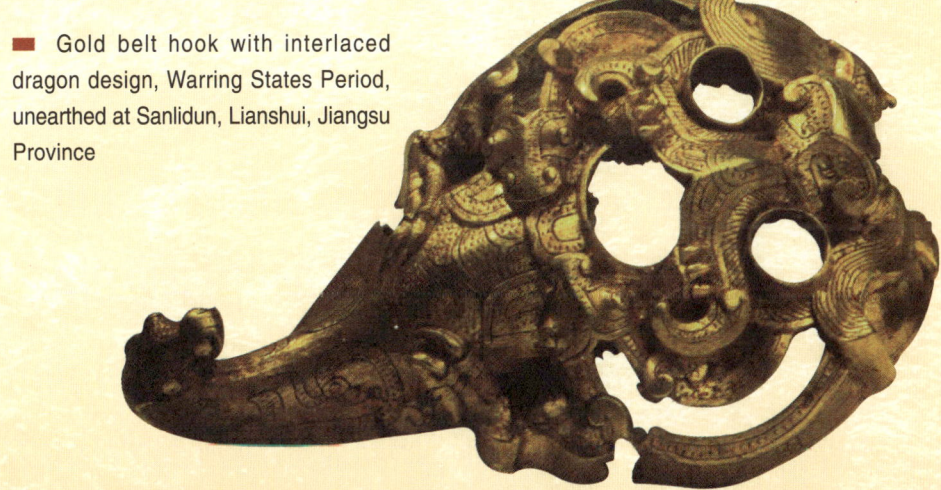

■ Gold belt hook with interlaced dragon design, Warring States Period, unearthed at Sanlidun, Lianshui, Jiangsu Province

The Story of Gold

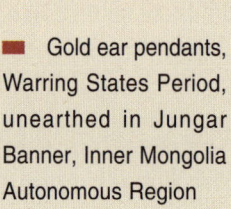

■ Gold ear pendants, Warring States Period, unearthed in Jungar Banner, Inner Mongolia Autonomous Region

ware. The dragons' eyes are unique in that they have pieces of turquoise inlaid in them. The elliptical gold end has a square mortise to fit with the straight handle and both the curved blade and the handle are made of iron. The use of gold in such items indicates that they were ornamental or ritual objects, and not practical weapons. It is possible that they were made specially to accompany the deceased in the afterlife. The large number of gold articles found in this tomb shows the high social status of the occupant.

The necklace from the tomb consists of a string of 908 gold beads, each with a diameter of about 0.15 cm.

The most precious gold objects found in this tomb are two waterfowl-shaped belt hooks and a gold belt hook in the form of coiled snakes. Such belt hooks were used by non-Han nationalities living in northern China at the time. One of them features a duck-like animal craning its neck, with a long beak, turquoise-inlaid eyes, dragon patterns on the breast and feather patterns on the back. Its partner has a similar bird with a flat body and S-shaped beak. The bird has dragon patterns on its back, which has 14 holes drilled in it and believed to have been for inlaying jade or other precious stones, now lost. The other hook features a coiled snake with four smaller ones on its back.

Belt hooks account for a large percentage of the gold ware found in tombs of the Spring and Autumn and Warring States periods.

Two gold belt hooks believed to be from the Warring States Period were found in a Western Han Dynasty tomb in February 1965 in Sanlidun, Lianshui County, Jiangsu Province. One of the hooks, seven cm long, is shaped liked a pipa, a traditional Chinese string instrument. Its top is in the form of an animal's head. There are two dragon patterns carved on the handle. The other one, 12 cm long, looks like a strange animal squatting with the front limbs raised to breast height.

Gold belt hooks have also been found in a tomb in Qufu, Shandong Province, and from the tomb of Marquis Yi of Zeng in Suixian County, Hubei Province. Belt hooks indicated the status of various ranks of feudal nobles, although there were no rules governing this common practice. It seems to have been the forerunner of the later practice of belts indicating the owner's rank.

■ Iron sword with gold handle, Spring and Autumn Period, found in Yimen Village, Baoji, Shaanxi Province

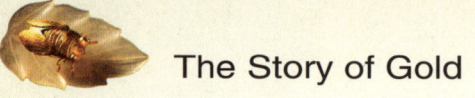

The Story of Gold

Xiongnu Gold Crown

It is notable that during the Spring and Autumn and Warring States Period, gold craftsmanship was highly developed among the non-Han nomadic tribes in northern China, at a level equal to or even better to that in the Central Plains area.

There were numerous nomadic tribes in the highlands of Shanxi and Shaanxi provinces and Inner Mongolia during the Shang and Zhou dynasties. They were often in contact with the peoples of the Central Plains in the forms of trade and warfare. They adopted the bronze culture of their neighbors, and made bronze knives with handles with horse-head patterns, spoons with snake-pattern decorations and daggers with tiger-patterns. The Xiongnus (Huns) were a powerful alliance of many of these tribes during the Warring States Period.

Many Xiongnu tombs have been discovered and excavated. Among the most important are the ones at Aluchaideng in Hanggin Banner, Xigoupan in Jungar Banner and Shihuigou in Ejin Horo Banner----all in the Inner Mongolia Autonomous Region; Nalingaotu in Shenmu County, Shaanxi Province, and Alagou in Toksun County, in the Xinjiang Uygur Autonomous Region. All the gold ware found in these tombs are ornaments for swords, horses and belts. No gold utensils have been unearthed. They also include necklaces, earrings, strings of beads, ornaments for hats and crowns, and decorative pieces and plates, with patterns of such animals as cows, sheep, horses, eagles, wolves and tigers. The patterns are all in realistic and natural styles, as seen on bronze wares found in this area during the Shang and Zhou dynasties.

The Xiongnu's gold ware demonstrates a high level of craftsmanship. What is more important is the impressive quantity and quality of the gold ware found in these tombs. A total of 218 gold items were found in the Aluchaideng tomb, with a total weight of over 4,000 g. An eagle-shaped gold crown is the most precious artifact of this hoard. It has a domed cap with bells and an eagle-shaped decoration, and fine and vividly designed patterns of animals. It is the earliest gold crown found in China.

Gold earrings, necklaces and decorative plates have been found in tombs at Xigoupan in Jungar Banner, Inner Mongolia. But, decorative strips of gold with various animal patterns account for most of the artifacts unearthed there. Two gold earrings were found in the tomb of a male, which

033
Spring and Autumn and Warring States Periods—The Early Years of Gold Luxury Goods

■ Gold cup with cloud design and a colander, Warring States Period, found in the tomb of Marquis Yi of Zeng in Suizhou, Hubei Province

The Story of Gold

shows that male Xiongnus wore earrings at that time. Of a similar shape to those found in Aluchaideng, these round earrings all have turquoise and trumpet-shaped decorations, proclaiming the owner's wealth and status.

In Talahao Township of Ih Ju League in Inner Mongolia, a decorative gold plate has been unearthed with a pattern of a tiger fighting a wolf. The complicated pattern in clear lines and the well-designed pattern of surrounding birds and animals make the artifact a treasure of the Spring and Autumn and Warring States era.

Unearthed in Shenmu County, Shaanxi Province, were gold ornaments in the shape of tiger and deer, both male and female. Different from those found in Inner Mongolia, these artifacts were made according to the shapes of the animals, and they are neither in a frame nor in a square shape. They were used as decorations for belts or hung on horses.

Round and strip-shaped pieces of gold with tiger patterns have been found in Xiongnu tombs in Alagou, Toksun County, in the Xinjiang Uygur Autonomous Region.

■ Waterfowl-shaped belt hooks, Spring and Autumn Period, unearthed at Yimen Village, Baoji, Shaanxi Province

Chapter 4
Gold Ware in Qin and Han Dynasties, and Its Magical Significance

It is said that in 316 BC, King Hui of the State of Qin sent armies to attack the State of Shu. He tricked the ruler of Shu into building a road between the two states and put five stone cows near the border, with some gold bars piled behind them. When it was reported to the ruler of Shu that the cows could produce gold bars, he ordered that they be brought to his capital. This involved building a road through the trackless waste which separated Shu from Qin, along which the army of the State of Qin marched into the State of Shu.

Tombs of the Qin Dynasty (221-206 BC) have yielded very few gold items. However, the Mausoleum of Qin Shihuangdi, the first emperor of united China, has never been excavated, and is believed to remain intact. According to historical records, a large number of gold wares were interred with the deceased.

■ Gold five-zhu (zhu is an ancient unit of weight, equal to 2.083 g) coin, Han Dynasty

The Story of Gold

Gold Ware of the Qin Dynasty

In the 1970s, part of the Mausoleum of Qin Shihuangdi was uncovered by accident. It was a pit containing hundreds of life-sized terra-cotta warriors, guarding the emperor's burial place. Among the artifacts found in this pit were 737 gold ornaments, including eight *danglu* (an ornament hung around a horse's neck). Bronze *danglu* were common in the Western Zhou Dynasty, but these were the first gold ones ever discovered.

A tomb dating from the Qin period in Lixian County, Gansu Province, yielded a wooden statue of a tiger covered with ten wrappings of gold foil. It is 41 cm long and three-four cm wide. Also found in the tomb were two owl-shaped gold ornaments and gold squares bearing various decorative patterns similar to those found on bronze wares of the Shang and Zhou dynasties.

In 1979, a silver plate with gold decorations was found in a Western Han Dynasty sacrificial burial pit in Wuotuo Village, Shandong Province. The gold patterns are those of dragons and phoenixes. Such plates became common in later times. An inscription of 47 characters carved along the outer rim announces that the plate, originally made in the State of Qi during the Warring States Period, had once been used in the Qin imperial palace. It is China's only gold-plated vessel with a Qin inscription.

Bronze fell out of favor round about this time, and the art of making gold objects shook off the influence of the bronze craftsmen, to become a fully independent art. In addition, a new stimulus to the production and processing of gold came when the Western Han Dynasty scholar Li Shaojun claimed that the use of gold and silver wares could lengthen one's life and improve one's health.

037
Gold Ware in Qin and Han Dynasties, and Its Magical Significance

■ Filigreed gold *tianlu* (a kind of mythical animal), Eastern Han Dynasty, found in the tomb of Liu Chang

The Story of Gold

Han Dynasty Jade Burial Suit Sewn with Fine Gold Threads

Gold continued to be associated with health, long life and even immortality—probably based on the fact that it is virtually indestructible—from Han times through the Wei (220-265) and Jin (265-420) dynasties. A gold oven used by alchemists to make so-called pills of immortality was found in Shapo Village, Xi'an, Shaanxi Province, and two jade burial suits sewn with fine gold threads and gold needles were found in the tomb of Liu Sheng, Prince Jing of the State of Zhongshan, in Mancheng, Hebei Province. The gold threads linking the jade pieces of the suits (one each for the prince and his wife) weigh a total of 1,800 g. Gold medicine containers have been found also dating from the Han period.

The importance attached to gold by the Han aristocracy is attested to *Records of the Historian*: "The state treasury contains more than 400,000 *jin* of gold." *The History of Former Han*, China's first dynastic history, informs us that "the ruler of Guanghan of the State of Shu liked gold and silver ware, and spent five million *liang* on each every year."

The emperors of the Western Han Dynasty often rewarded their subjects with gold and had large-sized gold coins made and circulated. Gold also accompanied Western Han aristocrats to their graves, as large quantities of the precious metal have been found in some 30 tombs of the period. The most important of these are the tombs of Liu Sheng in Mancheng, Hebei Province, Liu Xiu and Liu Chang in Dingxian County, also in Hebei Province, Liu Jing in Hanjiang, Jiangsu Province, the king of the State of Nanyue in Guangzhou, Guangdong Province and King Xiang of the State of Qi in Zibo, Shandong Province.

Historical records show that Guo Kuang, the younger brother of the empress of Emperor Guangwu, amassed over 100 million *liang* of gold. Guo was a believer in the current superstition that using gold utensils and even eating gold could ensure immortality. According to the records, "There are 400 servants in his family doing nothing but making gold objects, and the noise of their doing so spreads as far as the suburbs."

039
Gold Ware in Qin and Han Dynasties, and Its Magical Significance

■ Gold sheep with inlaid decoration, Eastern Han Dynasty, found in the tomb of Liu Chang, Dingzhou, Hebei Province

The Story of Gold

Gold Seals and the Seal Engraving Art of the Han Dynasty

Seals enjoy a long history in China. As early as in the Bronze Age, craftsmen would carve their names in a special way on the bronze wares they had made. Seals came into being in the Spring and Autumn Period. A silver seal now on display at the Tianjin Arts Museum dates from that era.

Seals soon came to be divided into official and private ones. Official seals were the symbol of official ranks and authority.

After unifying China, the Qin Dynasty set up a system for the use of official seals, with clear distinctions between those for officials of various ranks, including regulations on the materials used, and the shape of the knob and the seal, which had a special ribbon attached to it. Gold seals were mainly for high-ranking officials. This continued until the Sui Dynasty (581-618).

About 30 gold seals dating from the Han Dynasty have been unearthed, mainly from the tombs of kings and princes. Among the most important are the "Seal of Emperor Wen," "Seal of the King of the State of Dian," "Seal of King

Guangling" and a gold seal found in Japan, which was later found to have been a gift to a local ruler from a Chinese emperor.

The seal of Emperor Wen was found in the tomb of the king of the State of Nanyue, which flourished in Han times. The tomb is located on Mount Xianggang, in Guangzhou, Guangdong Province. With a weight of 148.5 g, it is the biggest gold seal so far found from that period. The inscription is in the so-called small script style. The surface is evenly divided into four square-shaped parts, with one Chinese letter in each part. This is a typical format of the seal calligraphy of the time.

The seal has a knob in the shape of a coiled dragon grasping the four corners of the top part with its claws. Cast in Nanyue, the seal was once owned by that state's second king, Zhao Mei. Neither Zhao Mei nor his predecessor Zhao Tuo submitted to the authority of the Han court; both of them were self claimed emperors—Zhao Mei as Emperor Wen and Zhao Tuo as Emperor Wu of Nanyue. Thus, Zhao Mei's seal reads "Seal of Emperor Wu." The third king of Nanyue, Zhao Yingqi, paid homage to the Western Han Dynasty, and was made a duke.

■ Jade suit sewn with gold thread, Western Han Dynasty, found in Western Han tomb in Mancheng, Hebei Province

The Story of Gold

In 1981, a gold seal was found in a brickyard in Ganquan Township, Hanjiang County, Jiangsu Province. Made of pure gold, the cubic seal weighs 123 g, and the knob is in the shape of a turtle. The inscription reads "Xi (Official Seal) of King Guangling."

King Guangling was Liu Jing, the ninth son of Liu Xiu, or Emperor Guangwu, the first emperor of the Eastern Han Dynasty (6 BC-57 AD). According to the *History of the Later Han Dynasty*, when Emperor Guangwu died in 157, his son Liu Zhuang came to the throne as Emperor Ming. The latter promoted Liu Jing to King Guangling. Liu Jing later committed suicide after an attempted usurpation.

The discovery of the seal of King Guangling ended a heated, 200-year-long argument over a gold seal unearthed near Fukuoka, Japan.

According to the *History of the Later Han Dynasty*, Emperor Guangwu presented a gold seal to the ruler of the Kingdom of Nara in Japan in 57. The inscription read "The king of the State of Nara, Han Dynasty." The seal was found in 1784 near Fukuoka, which was claimed to be the one presented by Emperor Guangwu. However, scholars widely denounced it as a fake. Then, when the seal of King Guangling was found in China and compared with the one in Japan, they were found to have come from the same workshop, confirming the authenticity of the latter and indicating the close diplomatic relations some 2,000 years ago between the two countries. The seal of King Guangling and the seal of the King of the State of Dian were once taken to Japan to be displayed with the gold seal found in Fukuoka.

The wide use of seals from the Han Dynasty onward

gradually made seal engraving an important genre of Chinese calligraphy, and seal engraving became an independent art.

Seal engraving was highly developed in the Han Dynasty, with various styles in fashion. The inscription on the seal of the prime minister of the Kingdom of Langya, believed to be from the later stage of the dynasty, is famed for its rich and exuberant style, with square characters written in virile strokes. The seal of Marquis Guanzhong, with typical square characters, is in a graceful and flowing style. The seal of General Pingdong of the State of Wei during the Three Kingdoms Period is in one of the Han Dynasty styles.

The characters on the gold seal of Marquis Guiyi of Xianbei, of the Jin Dynasty, are written in forceful strokes. They are seal characters, but betray some elements of the official script.

Gold Ware in Qin and Han Dynasties, and Its Magical Significance

■ Horseshoe-shaped gold ingots, Han Dynasty, unearthed at Yuhua Village, Xi'an, Shaanxi Province

The Story of Gold

Han Dynasty Gold Coins

Gold currency in tablet form was minted in the State of Chu in southern China during the Spring and Autumn Period. Such objects have been found in many locations originally within the state's vast territory south of the Yangtze River and even some areas north of the country's longest river. Gold disks from the Spring and Autumn Period have been found in the Shizi (Lion) Mountain near Shaoxing in Zhejiang Province. They are of different sizes, but are of the same thickness, and some of the bigger ones' rims had been cut, indicating that they were units of currency, which needed to be cut and weighed for various payments.

In the Qin and Han dynasties, there were two categories of currency—gold and bronze ingots. The former was mostly used by the wealthy for large payments, while the latter was mainly used by ordinary people for small purchases. There were three types of gold currency in the Han Dynasty, known as *jinbing*, or gold ingots, with a thickness of one-two cm and a diameter of seven-eight cm, U-shaped gold ingots and *linzhi* gold ingots, shaped like a horse's hoof. Thirty-six such ingots, weighing a total of 3,000 g, were found in Jiangsu Province in 1982, together with a gold figure of an animal weighing 9,000 g. The latter is 10.2 cm high, 16 cm long and 17.8 cm wide. It looks like a leopard, and has a collar.

045
Gold Ware in Qin and Han Dynasties, and Its Magical Significance

■ Gold bars, Western Han Dynasty, found in a Western Han tomb, Mancheng, Hebei Province

The Story of Gold

Funeral Objects from Officials' Tombs

The popularity of the superstition from Han times on that the use of gold utensils and other objects could prolong life or even convey immortality led to the practice of burying gold objects with the dead, in the hope of easing the transition to the afterlife. An impressive amount of gold objects and silver wares with gold inlay have been found in more than 30 tombs of Han Dynasty princes and dukes.

In the tomb of Liu Sheng, famous for the two gold-threaded jade burial suits, was found a set of 12 gold objects, including four gold acupuncture needles in three types.

Eighty gold objects were found in the tomb of Liu Chang in Dingxian County, Hebei Province. One is in the shape of a dragon, and another is in the shape of a mythical auspicious animal looking like a tiger called a *bixie*. There are also gold models of sheep. All these items were manufactured using a special technique called "thread piling."

There are two *bixie*, fixed on a flat stand decorated with a pattern of flowing clouds and grain. One has two horns, while the other has only one. The eyes are inlaid with turquoise. There are inlays of agate and turquoise on the front of the neck, the back and other parts of the body, which is made of fine gold chips and decorated with a thread-piled pattern of feathers and grain.

The similarity in design and workmanship of these objects suggests that they were made by the same craftsman.

■ Gold-plated silver basin, Qin Dynasty, found in Dawu Township, Zibo City, Shandong Province

The Story of Gold

■ Gold ear pendants, Han Dynasty, excavated at Yulin, Jilin Province

The gold ware found in the tomb of Liu Jing in Hanjiang, Jiangsu Province, can be taken as representative of such products manufactured in southern China. The gold ornaments are in the shape of a dragon's head, crown, shield, triangle and globe. The most interesting is the dragon's head. The eyes, nose, horns, teeth, whiskers and scales were made by thread-piling or with gold grains.

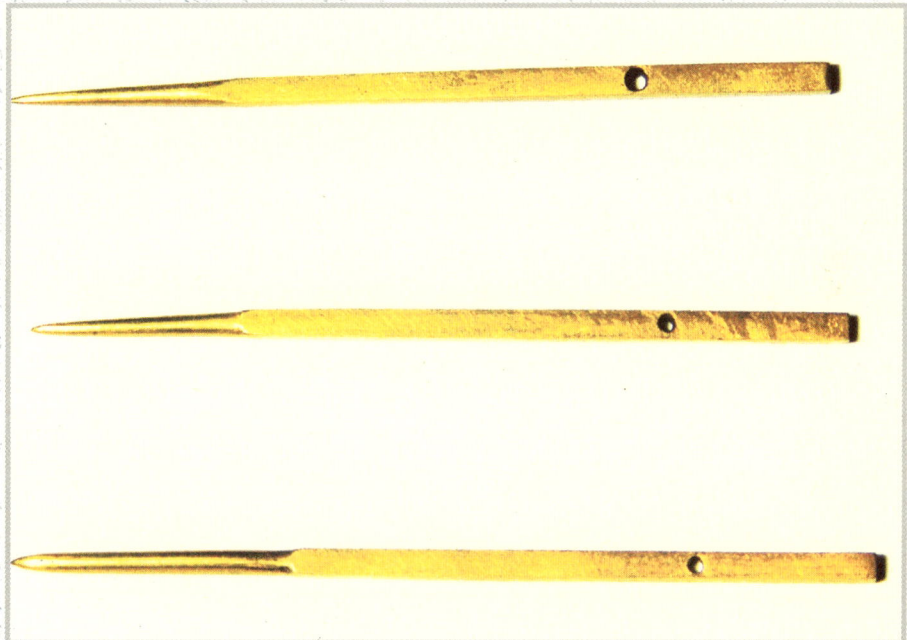

■ Gold needles, Western Han Dynasty, found in the tomb of the King of Zhongshan, Mancheng, Hebei Province

The Story of Gold

Some gold and silver wares, mainly plate-shaped ornaments and jewelry, have also been found in various locations of north and northwest China, including a group of Xianbei tombs in Laoheshen, Yushu County, Jilin Province. The tombs, of nomadic tribesmen, date from the Han Dynasty. A necklace found in one of the tombs consists of 266 orange agate beads, and six golden tubes separate groups of beads. An ear pendant has five rows of vertical decorations made of gold, including a peach leaf and five miniature gold leafs in the shape of *gui* (a ceremonial object). A gold plate found in Qilian County, Qinghai Province, is decorated with scene of wolves attacking a cow in relief.

A unique ornament now on display at the Tianjin Arts Museum has Ordos cultural characteristics. It consists of three parts—a figure of a tiger as the upper part, be-

■ Gold dragon, Eastern Han Dynasty, found in the tomb of Liu Chang

low which is a sheep, and finally a ring hanging from the sheep's mouth.

With the development of the Silk Road, starting in the Han Dynasty, Western techniques of working in gold were introduced to China along the road. This ancient trade route between China and the Mediterranean Sea extended some 6,440 km, linking China with the Roman Empire. The Silk Road was pioneered by Zhang Qian, an envoy of Western Han Dynasty Emperor Wu to the Western Regions, which included what is now the Xinjiang Uygur Autonomous Region in Northwest China and the ancient states of Central Asia. The Silk Road had an epoch-making significance for trade and cultural exchanges between the East and the West. Large amounts of silk, porcelain, and gold and silver ware were exported westward along this route, as far as Persia and the Roman Empire. And Western products as gold and silver objects, precious stones, agate and diamonds, not to mention the Buddhist religion made their way to China, introducing the culture and crafts of the West to China, including new gold-working techniques, starting about the first century BC. Gold and silver ornaments manufactured with such introduced techniques as wire-inlaying and thread-piling have been found in some Eastern Han Dynasty tombs. One such ornament, a gold finger ring found in an Eastern Han tomb on Xianlie Road, Guangzhou, Guangdong Province, has an agate inlay clearly featuring a Western style. At the same time, Chinese gold and silver products were exported to the west. A gold belt was found in 1939 in Alma-ata, a city in

051
Gold Ware in Qin and Han Dynasties, and Its Magical Significance

The Story of Gold

Kazakhstan. It has a decorative pattern of a supernatural being riding a mythical animal, and is in typical Han Dynasty style.

■ Gold mythical animal, Han Dynasty, found in Nanyao Village, Xuyi, Jiangsu Province

Chapter 5
Objects with Western Characteristics from the Wei and Jin and Southern and Northern Dynasties Periods

■ Gold hat ornament, Northern Dynasties, found in Shunyi, Beijing

The Story of Gold

Gold Collections of the Aristocracy

With the fall of the Han Dynasty, China once more endured a period of division and clashes between rival political powers. This lasted through the period of the Three Kingdoms, Jin and Southern and Northern Dynasties (220-589). In the north, the Great Wall, fortified during the Qin and Han dynasties, failed to stop invasions by the nomadic tribes living in northern China, who conquered large tracts south of the Great Wall.

However, the turbulence of the times does not seem to diminish the avarice of the aristocratic classes, some of whom even kept private workshops where gold and silver objects were turned out by master craftsmen for the exclusive enjoyment of their masters. According to the *Buddhist Temples in Luoyang* by Yang Xuanzhi of Northern Wei, Yuan Chen, the king of Hejian, took delight in showing off his collection of gold and silver objects which he had had specially made. Many of them were connected with horses, of which Yuan Chen was an aficionado, and included a silver-cast manger, more than 100 gold bottles and silver cauldrons, and a host of gold and silver wine sets. The mania for such luxuries led one of the Northern Wei emperors to ban the employment of private gold craftsmen, fearing social unrest. The decree seems to have gone unheeded, however.

No gold works of outstanding artistry have been found from this period, but a large number of ordinary gold vessels and jewelry were manufactured, such as gold finger rings, bracelets, necklaces, ear-rings, ear-drops, short and long hairpins, and such animal figures as dogs, mandarin ducks, galloping horses and unicorns. Also manufactured were traditional ornamental gold strips and plates, which were particularly popular in the areas in both Southern and Northern China where minority peoples lived. A total of 129 such items were found in an early Eastern Jin Dynasty tomb in Nanjing, Jiangsu Province. Also found in large amounts

055
Objects with Western Characteristics from the Wei and Jin and Southern and Northern Dynasties Periods

■ Gold auspicious beast, Northern Wei Dynasty, found in Horqin Left Wing Middle Banner, Inner Mongolia Autonomous Region

The Story of Gold

have been gold seals. Found in a Three Kingdoms tomb in Ezhou, Hubei Province, were 47 gold objects' including mandarin ducks and beads. Gold beads were found in a Jin Dynasty tomb in Changsha, Hunan Province. The hollow beads are in various shapes, with mini gold beads attached to the surface of some, and others inlaid with rubies and emeralds. From a Southern Dynasty tomb in Luoding County, Guangdong Province, a gold bracelet and a gold finger ring were unearthed. Head ornaments have also been found in wide areas of southern China, including Jiangsu and Jiangxi provinces.

Eastern Jin Dynasty gold objects have been found in southern Jiangsu, including long and short hairpins among 25 gold objects found in the tomb of Wang Danhu in Nanjing. Found in the tomb of Wang Yi, also in Nanjing, were such objects as a finger ring inlaid with diamonds, and gold cups and bells.

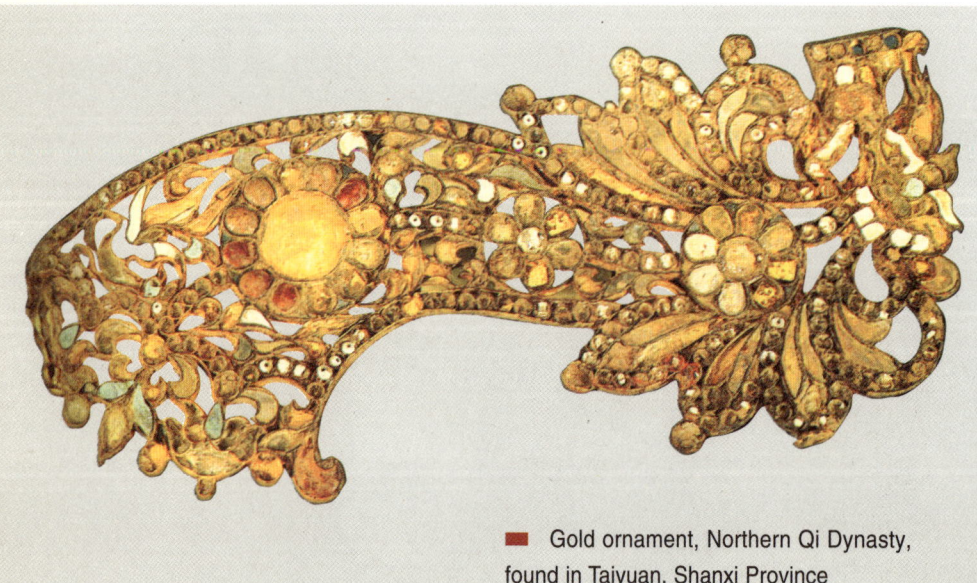

■ Gold ornament, Northern Qi Dynasty, found in Taiyuan, Shanxi Province

■ Gold hollow-cored flower beads, Jin Dynasty, found in the Li Family Mansion, Changsha, Hunan Province

057

Objects with Western Characteristics from the Wei and Jin and Southern and Northern Dynasties Periods

Particularly interesting are two gold seals found in Liangcheng, Inner Mongolia. They belonged to nobles of the Xianbei tribe, and have the characters *guiyi* engraved on the surface, which means to submit to the authority of somebody, and is thought to indicate the subordinate status of the owners to the Han emperor. Also found in Inner Mongolia and Liaoning Province were gold crowns in the shape of the top of a tree, with gold branches and leaves which would rock and sway as the wearer moved. The crowns belonged to Xianbei nobles, and seem to have been copied from those worn by rulers of the Han and Wei dynasties.

The Story of Gold

Utensils and Vessels with a Foreign Flavor

The few gold vessels found so far dating from the Wei, Jin and the Southern and Northern Dynasties mostly bear traces of the influence of the style of the Sassanid Dynasty of Persia (224-636).

In 1981, a silver plate coated with gold was found in a Northern Wei Dynasty tomb near Datong, Shanxi Province. It was hammered and pressed into shape, and has engraved decorative patterns typical of the products of Sassanid craftsmen. The figure of a hunter on the plate

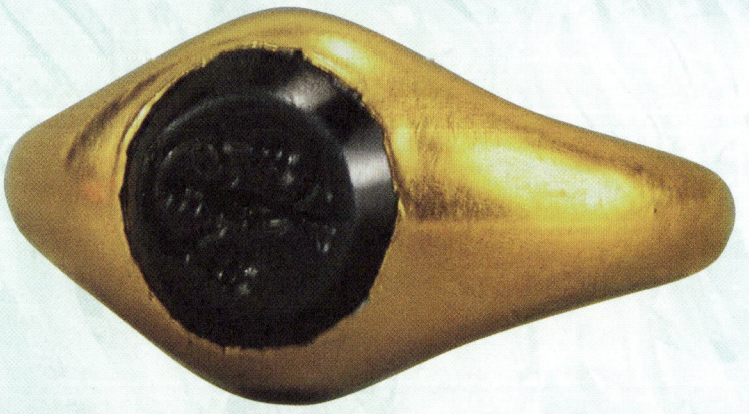

■ Gold ring, Jin Dynasty, found in the tomb of Li Xian, Guyuan, Ningxia Hui Autonomous Region

Gold seal of Marquis Guiyi of the Xianbei Ethnic Group, Western Jin Dynasty, unearthed at Liangcheng, Inner Mongolia Autonomous Region

has typical Persian features, dress and ornaments. He is spearing a boar which has just dashed out of the undergrowth.

Another example of foreign influence on Chinese gold work in this period is a type of kettle called *Hu* (foreign, meaning from the Western regions) Kettle. One of these was found in the Northern Zhou Dynasty tomb of Li Xian and his wife, of Northern Zhou, in southern Guyuan County, Ningxia Hui Autonomous Region. The gold-plated silver vessel has a long neck, leg supports and a belly-like body. The top part of the handle is in the shape of a high-nosed man wearing a crown, and there are similar groups of figures, both male and female, around the kettle's body in a scene believed to originate from an ancient Greek tale.

Found in the same tomb was a gold finger ring, inlaid with a blue-and-gray precious stone. On the round surface of the precious stone is engraved the figure of a man holding what looks like scales. The style of the pattern indicates that the object originated in the West.

A necklace found in the tomb of Li Jingxun, the daughter of a high-ranking official of the Sui Dynasty, in Xi'an, Shaanxi Province, has been identified as being from west-

The Story of Gold

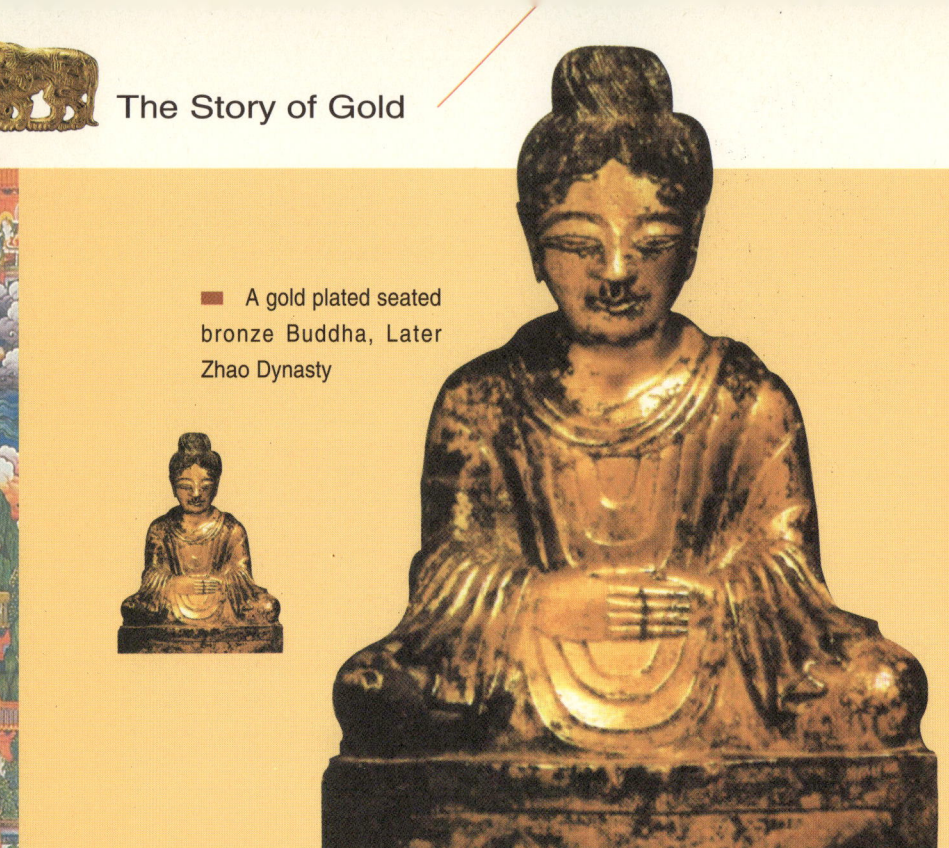

■ A gold plated seated bronze Buddha, Later Zhao Dynasty

ern Asia. It is the finest ancient necklace so far found in China.

There are 28 giant gold "beads" on the necklace, divided evenly into two groups and linked with a gold thread. Each of the beads is made up of 12 miniature gold rings, and inlaid with ten small pearls. On the upper part of the necklace is a round clasp inlaid with a light-blue sapphire. On either side of the clasp are round decorations, then beads, and then two square plates also inlaid with sapphires. At the lower part of the necklace is a T-shaped combination of ornaments. At the center is a round ornament inlaid with bloodstone which, in turn, inlaid with 24 pearls and attached with gold beads on fringes. On each side is a square plate inlaid with a sapphire. Connected with the edges of the plates are two round decorations each inlaid with a sapphire and surrounded by ten pearls. Hanging under the central plate is a large, egg-shaped and semi-transparent precious stone.

Judging by these finds, it was in this period that a combination of Western and Chinese styles appeared on gold objects. The Buddhist figures especially continue to show heavy Western influence. In the Tang Dynasty, gold vessels and bronze mirrors demonstrate a harmonious mixture of Chinese and Western cultures. Patterns of grapes, honeysuckles and lotuses—all typical of Persian decoration—are balanced with traditional Chinese images of auspicious birds and beasts, including unicorns, and dominate the decorative patterns on gold vessels of the dynasty.

061

Objects with Western Characteristics from the Wei and Jin and Southern and Northern Dynasties Periods

■ Gold crown decorated with spangles, Southern and Northern Dynasties, found in Darhan Muminggan Joint Banner, Ulanqab League, Inner Mongolia Autonomous Region

The Story of Gold

The Coming of Buddhism

Buddhist statues were brought into China as early as during the Eastern Han Dynasty. But, the major ones discovered so far date mainly from the Southern and Northern Dynasties Period, when Buddhism reached the height of its influence at the courts of the rulers.

A rectangular gold Buddhist plaque was found in an Eastern Jin Dynasty tomb in Zhenjiang, Jiangsu Province. The naked standing Buddhist figure has a child's face, with its head surrounded by a halo and its arms outstretched. The figure is believed to be that of the newly-born Sakyamuni, the founder of Buddhism, and the plaque is assumed to have come from the West.

■ Gold thimble, Northern Dynasties, found in Shunyi, Beijing

■ Gilded silver plate, Southern and Northern Dynasties, unearthed at Xiaozhan Village Datong, Shanxi Province

063
Objects with Western Characteristics from the Wei and Jin and Southern and Northern Dynasties Periods

A gold-plated statue of a seated Buddha made in the fourth year (338) of the rule of Emperor Jianwu of the Later Zhou Dynasty. The 39.7-cm-high statue is now in the collection of the San Francisco Art Gallery. Its base is decorated with Western-inspired cloud patterns. A gold-plated bronze Buddhist statue unearthed at Xi'an in 1979 has triangular and diamond-shaped patterns. Specialists date it to the fourth century, and think that it was made by a Chinese craftsman who had been influenced by Western techniques.

Gold objects from this period with religious symbols include gold wafers found in the tomb of Princess Ruru, the daughter-in-law of Prime Minister Gao Huan of Eastern Wei, in Cixian County, Hebel Province. The wafers carry detailed lotus patterns, flying Apsaras (Buddhist fairies),

The Story of Gold

Huasheng Tongzi (young boys sitting or standing on a lotus flower) and lucky birds surrounded by patterns of honeysuckles. The pattern lines are made of fine gold threads, soldered with small gold beads and inlaid with pearls, precious stones and amber. Honeysuckles appear for the first time in Chinese art at that time. From then on, honeysuckles, lotuses and flying Apsaras became standard elements of Buddhist art in China.

The introduction of Buddhism and related arts greatly affected China's gold ware production and the increase of varieties. Separate from vessels for daily use, ornaments and currency, Buddhist products gradually became, from the Wei and Jin dynasties on, an independent and even a major category of gold ware.

■ Gold galloping horse, Northern Wei Dynasty, found in Horqin Left Wing Middle Banner, Inner Mongolia Autonomous Region

Chapter 6
Tang Dynasty, the Heyday of Gold Artistry

T he Tang Dynasty marked the zenith of gold wares in China, in terms of varieties, shapes, superb craftsmanship and exquisite decorative patterns.

There was competition among officials and others to present gold and silver objects to the emperors, who, in turn, often awarded officials and meritorious subjects with such objects. It is recorded that Emperor Xuanzong (712-756) gave An Lushan, a favorite high-ranking general who later rebelled against the Tang court, a large number of gold and silver vessels on the latter's birthday. A high demand for gold vessels accompanied the dynasty's prosperity and flourishing economy, and stimulated the growth of gold craftsmanship.

This progress in gold artistry in turn boosted other handicrafts, such as bronze ware, lacquer ware and porcelain.

■ Gold comb, Tang Dynasty, unearthed in Yangzhou, Jiangsu Province

The Story of Gold

Property of the Rich and Powerful

Different from previous dynasties, Tang gold ware production focused on vessels and ornaments. The former were manufactured in great numbers and in a wide variety, including items connected with food and wine, medicine, cosmetics, sanitary use, and religious and funeral purposes.

The Tang Dynasty rulers, continuing the tradition which had started in the Qin Dynasty, regularly took so-called pills of immortality prepared by alchemists. Ordinary alchemists used ceramic or pottery stoves to prepare their pills and potions, but those working for the emperors and the aristocracy used stoves and other tools made of gold. Such stoves have been found in Hejia Village, Xi'an, Shaanxi Province. Together with them were discovered placer gold, gold powder, crystal, amethyst, amber and coral—all used in alchemical preparations. There was also a medicine box with dosing notes.

Dining sets and wine sets were the major categories of Tang Dynasty gold vessels. These treasures were shown off at grand banquets held by senior officials and other members of the aristocracy, to announce their owners' wealth and status. But, at the same time, it was widely believed that dining off gold plates and drinking from gold cups was conducive to a long life.

In fact, very few bowls and plates were made of pure gold; most were gold-plated or had decorative patterns of gold inlay. The plates were round, diamond-shaped, or in the form of a flowering crabapple or sunflower.

■ Gold-plated silver tea kettle, Tang Dynasty, found in Famen Temple, Fufeng, Shaanxi Province

The Story of Gold

Most of the 270 gold and silver objects unearthed at Hejia Village, Xi'an, in 1970 are food and drink sets, many of them rare and fine products. One of them is a hammered-out gold bowl with patterns of Chinese mandarin ducks and lotus leaves. On the outer surface there are two layers of decorative patterns of lotus leaves, the upper layer and the lower one, each with ten leaves. On the upper layer leaves are parrot, mandarin duck, deer, fox, rabbit and river deer figures, with decorative surroundings of branches, leaves and flowers. On the lower layer of lotus leaves are patterns of honeysuckles. On the outer surface of the bowl's round stand are flower patterns while on the inner surface are figures of mandarin ducks flying among flowers. The decorative patterns cover almost the entire outer surface.

Unearthed at the same time were four pure-gold cups and several gilded silver cups.

A famous Tang Dynasty kettle is one discovered at Hejia Village. It is made of silver, and there is a figure of a prancing horse holding a cup in its mouth on each side of the kettle. The fine patterning is all gilt. The kettle was part of a wine set used by the emperor, and is evidence for a claim in historical records that a horse was decorated with gold and silver ornaments for the celebrations of Tang Emperor Xuanzong's birthday on August 5 every year. The horse would dance to the imperial orchestra, and at the end of the performance perform a kowtow to the emperor, holding a wine cup in its mouth.

Tea and Buddhism

Tea has a long history in China, and tea drinking became very fashionable in the Tang Dynasty, when it became an elaborate ceremonial. A complete tea set was found in the basement of the pagoda in Famen Temple in Fufeng County, Shaanxi Province.

The set includes a reticulated gilded cage for baking tea. It was made of two parts—the body, with 15 flying swan geese and the cover, with 24, all in pairs. The build of the cage led scholars to the conclusion that both body and the cover were mould cast.

069
Tang Dynasty, the
Heyday of Gold Artistry

■ Pure-gold bowl with carved design, Tang Dynasty, unearthed at Hejia Village, Xi'an, Shaanxi Province

The Story of Gold

Also unearthed was a cage of similar function manufactured with gold and silver threads, in a unique craft.

For rolling dried tea pack into powder, a rolling set was needed, which consisted of a base, a tilting rolling slot and the roller. The set found in the Famen Temple was made by Wensiyuan, a royal workshop. It has a weight mark engraved so that no one could illegally replace the original with a fake and lighter one.

The tea drinking set also includes a container for the salt to be put into the boiled tea. The container has various decorative patterns over the surface. At the top of the cover was the pattern of a wisdom pearl, surrounded by two layers of lotus leaves decorated with dahlia head figures, which was a mark of Buddhist culture on a tea drinking set. Engraved around each of the four outlets was a scene with human figures such as the one in which a man is kneeling on a pad and playing a reed-pipe (Chinese wind instrument), with a phoenix flying around, a second scene in which a man is kneeling on a pad and playing traditional instrument lute and another scene in which a man is playing a vertical bamboo flute while another man is holding a Buddhist alms bowl by his side. These scenes feature harmonious mixture of Chinese concepts and Buddhist influence. Cranes, phoenix, snakes and pearls are all traditional Chinese luck marks, lute, the reed-pipe wind instrument and vertical bamboo flute are often used by scholars and scholar-officials while kneeling on pads and the alms bowl are out-and-out Buddhist. To put all these elements into one scene sends out a meaningful and clear signal, that is to put Buddhist elements into the pursue of a simple and primitive life mixed with the true nature. This is just the true spirit brought about by the tea culture. The gilt vessels on the other hand bring people back to the actual world, with a feeling of wealth and satisfaction. With all these combined as one and with the set buried underground in such an influential Buddhist temple, it came out a meaningful shot and a real wonder!

The precious objects, including the tea set, found in the basement of the Famen Temple pagoda have been identified as gifts specially made at the imperial workshop known as Wensiyuan and presented to the temple by the

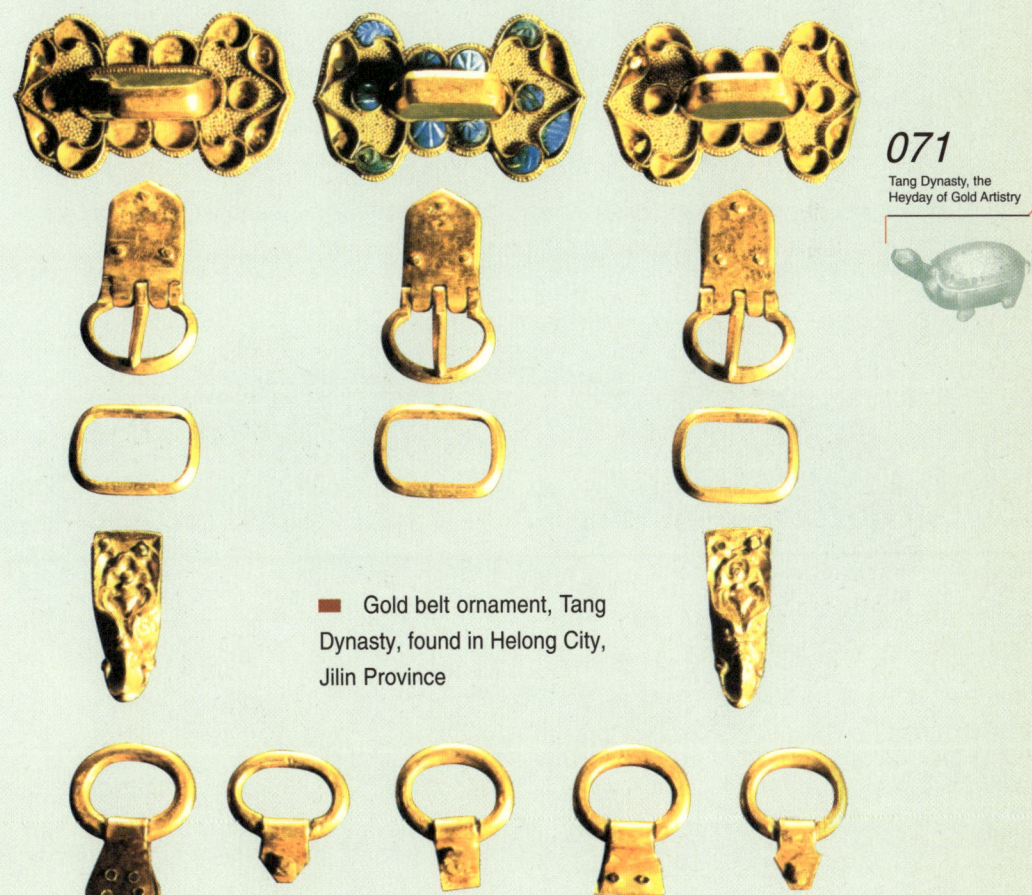

■ Gold belt ornament, Tang Dynasty, found in Helong City, Jilin Province

The Story of Gold

Tang emperors Yizong (860-874) and Xizong (874-888), both of whom were ardent believers in Buddhism. The hoard includes a gold-plated silver staff, a gold stupa for Buddhist relics, an eight-layer treasure box—two of which are gold-plated and three of pure gold—a silver stick with decorative gold plate and a statue of Bodhisattva. There are also four bone fragments thought to be parts of the Buddha's finger bones.

The gold-plated silver staff is the only one of its kind so far discovered in China. It was carried by an abbot as a symbol of his status. The top of the stick is shaped like four peaches, each with three rings hanging from it. The four peaches indicate four truths (catur-satyas) and 12 principal and subsidiary causes of Buddhism.

Gold or gold-plated objects connected with Buddhism have also been found in Heilongjiang, Jiangsu and Gansu provinces.

■ Silver plate with inlaid design, Tang Dynasty, found in Xi'an, Shaanxi Province

Gold Objects Presented to the Tang Emperors

During the reign of Tang Emperor Daizong (762-779), both court and local officials sent gifts to the ruler on the occasions of four festivals—New Year's Day, the Dragon Boat Festival (the fifth day of the fifth lunar month), the Winter Solstice (the 22nd of the 24 solar terms) and the emperor's birthday. During Emperor Dezong's reign (779-805), such gifts were sent on a monthly or even daily basis, and became part of the emperor's two private treasuries called Qionglin and Daying. It was mainly the value of these presents that ensured an official's promotion.

Some objects believed to be part of this system, and sent by officials in southern China, have been found among artifacts found in northern China. A silver basin with a gold-plated pattern of mandarin ducks found in the cellar of the Famen Temple bears an inscription identifying its place of origin as western Zhejiang. The patterns on its inner and outer surfaces perfectly match each other, showing a high level of gold craftsmanship in southern China during the Tang Dynasty. A plate with gold-plated fish and lotus patterns, found in Xi'an was sent to the Tang emperor by

073
Tang Dynasty, the
Heyday of Gold Artistry

The Story of Gold

Regional Inspector Li Mian of Hongzhou Prefecture in what is now Nanchang, Jiangxi Province. Other articles of tribute sent to the Tang emperors are a gold-plated dish with deer patterns presented by Regional Inspector Liu Zan of Xuanzhou and a silver plate with gold-plated engraved flower patterns, presented by Salt and Iron Transport Commissioner Jing Hui.

According to historical records, Wang Bo, military commissioner of the Huainan region, sent a total of 5,900 gold and silver objects on three occasions to Emperor Wenzong (827-840).

■ Gold-plated silver salt jar, Tang Dynasty, found in Famen Temple

The Aesthetics of Gold

The women of the Tang Dynasty were fonder of gold ornaments and utensils than women of any other dynasties. Numerous fine Tang ornaments have been found in Heilongjiang, Liaoning, Jilin, Zhejiang, Jiangsu, Hubei, Ningxia and Guangdong, which include earrings, finger rings, hair ornaments and bracelets. These gold ornaments are better than those manufactured in earlier dynasties in terms of shape, design and style. The fine characteristics of Tang ornaments had an obvious impact on gold craftsmanship of the Song and Yuan dynasties.

Hairpins found in the tomb of Yang, a concubine of the king of Wu in the Tang Dynasty, in Anlu County, Hubei Province are made of gold threads as fine as hairs coiled in exquisite patterns. One has peach patterns in three layers. Another has a plum blossom pattern, together with the image of a pair of birds, surrounded by hexagon gold chips. Also found in the tomb was a gold hairpin with sunflower patterns. In Helong County, Jilin Province, two plain U-shaped gold hairpins have been found dating from Tang times.

The Story of Gold

■ Gold-plated silver ewer, Tang Dynasty, found in Famen Temple

Women in the Tang Dynasty also liked earrings. In Yangzhou, Jiangsu Province, four gold earrings from this period were found, and two of them look similar, each consisting of three parts. Found in Helong County, Jilin Province was a pair of round gold earrings with no decorative patterns on their well-polished surfaces.

Three gold finger rings were also excavated in Yangzhou. One of them has a polished surface without a decorative pattern. Another has an oval hole inlaid with a precious stone. The third also has an oval hole, but the precious stone is missing. Among other decorations are petals, with the surrounding receptacles inlaid with pieced pearls which are linked to gold wires. A thick gold finger ring found in a Tang Dynasty tomb in Shuangta District, Chaoyang City, Liaoning Province has a polished surface without any decorative pattern. A gold finger ring found in Yingde, Guangdong Province, has a semicircular cross-section. Bracelet is an arm or wrist adornment.

A broken bracelet found in Helong County, Jilin Province, is 19.5 cm long, weighs 69 g, and has no decoration on the polished surface. A bracelet found in the cellar of Famen Temple has gold-plated image of Vajna club (thunderbolt) surrounded by lotus petals. Found in Sanyuan Road, Yangzhou, Jiangsu Province was a gold *zhi* (fine-toothed comb sometimes used as a headgear). It has intricate patterns engraved on the handle, including images of plum blossoms and bees. Engraved in the center is a pair of flying Apsaras playing musical instruments.

Decorative Patterns

Tang Dynasty gold objects were famed not only for their richness of variety and shape, but also for their exquisite decorative patterns. The images include those of animals, plants, and people engaged in such activities as hunting, playing music and holding Buddhist ceremonies. The patterns feature symmetrical and harmonious placing, creating an inner rhythm. Especially the matching between the patterns and the shapes of the objects shows that Tang craftsmen had a highly mature aes-

The Story of Gold

thetic sense and capability of artistic expression. Images of turtles and foxes imply a prayer for peace, and a mandarin duck holding a ribbon in its mouth implies a prayer for a harmonious marriage and longevity. Roses indicate wealth, and honeysuckles, lotuses and pomegranates are symbols of social prosperity.

Some of the decorative patterns are taken from scenes of daily life, such as hunting, children playing and horses prancing, indicating that the owners of these objects lived amid scenes of peace and harmony.

■ Tortoise-shaped tea container, Tang Dynasty, found in Famen Temple

Cream of the Prosperous Tang Dynasty

With the establishment of the Tang Dynasty, the Silk Road was reopened and maritime trade flourished. The Tang capital Chang'an (now Xi'an) became a magnet for traders, Buddhist monks, scholars, tourists and potentates from all over the world. These widespread exchanges with other cultures are reflected in the gold wares of the dynasty.

Tang Dynasty gold objects from the middle of the eighth century already show the influence of the central and western Asian areas, as Chinese craftsmen began to copy the styles of imported gold objects. Some of the gold wares used in the Tang Dynasty were imported from central or western Asia, some were imitations of such objects, and others featured a combination of Chinese and foreign styles. Some early products of the latter were awkward, as they simply combined Western shapes with Chinese patterns or they had Chinese patterns mixed with Western ones. For example, the shape of a gold-plated goblet with typical Chinese patterns of mandarin ducks and grass is a typical Byzantine concept. A gold cup with a Capricorn pattern

The Story of Gold

shows Persian and Indian influences.

Gradually, Chinese gold craftsmen stopped simply imitating foreign shapes and patterns, and created a new style in which extraneous elements were harmonized with Chinese traditions.

Some 300 pieces made in the mid-Tang period have been found, and more than 1,200 have been discovered dating from the later stage. Chinese-style decorative patterns of phoenixes and unicorns mingle unobtrusively with foreign patterns such as grapes, honeysuckles and twin lotus flowers on one stalk. Some foreign patterns which appear on early-Tang gold objects had been discarded by the end of the dynasty. However, such Western Asian techniques as hammer-pressing were adopted and further developed by Chinese craftsmen.

From a broader perspective, the development of gold working in the Tang Dynasty reflects the maturing of the Chinese psychology. The previous tendency of following traditional concepts and ideas slavishly began to be abandoned for a process of cultivating a broad and tolerant mentality. So, the traces of foreign cultures on individual arts and crafts are a meaningful symbol of changes in mentality and ideology.

■ Gold filigreed knife with a diamond-shaped handle, Tang Dynasty, found in a Tang Dynasty tomb in Anlu, Hubei Province

Emergence of the South

The Dingmao Bridge in Dantu County, Runzhou, located by the ancient Grand Canal, was an important gold and silver ware production center in southern China. The renowned Tang Dynasty poet Li Bai vividly describes the flourishing scene in one of his poems. According to the history book *The New Book of the Tang Dynasty*, southern China was the main source of the gold and silver objects which were sent as gifts by officials to the emperors. Most of the silver and gold objects of the late Tang Dynasty so far unearthed were from the area south of the Yangtze and Huaihe rivers. In the area of Dingmao Bridge alone, more than 900 such objects have been unearthed, including a wine set with an image of a turtle bearing on its back the *Analects of Confucius* and a jade candle holder. More than 100 gold items were found in the tomb of the concubine of the king of the State of Wu, which was subordinate to the Tang Dynasty, in the Wangzi Mountains, Anlu County, Hubei Province. Some 100 late-Tang silver wares, including some gold-plated ones, were unearthed at Changxing, Zhejiang Province, and some gold-plated hair ornaments

081
Tang Dynasty, the
Heyday of Gold Artistry

The Story of Gold

were unearthed at Huangdigang, Guangzhou, Guangdong Province.

The wine set has a turtle-shaped base, which includes a hollow for a drinker's wager chips. Unearthed at the same time were 50 gold-plated silver chips with an inscription of the game to be played with them and quotations from the *Analects of Confucius*. The gold-plated turtle has its head raised and looks as if it is in motion.

In the same location was found a gold-plated box with the Chinese characters *li shi* (strong man) engraved on the bottom. This might be an early brand name. This is backed up by the Chinese characters *yuzhang lishi* engraved on a porcelain jar, believed to be one of the famous items displayed in the boat-shaped Wangchun Tower in Chang'an for the emperor and court officials.

The prominence of the gold ware of south China during the mid-to-late Tang Dynasty was linked to the southward shift of China's economic center, which, together with the northward thrust of southern Chinese culture, was characteristic of this dynasty and the following Song Dynasty.

■ Gold tea grinder, Tang Dynasty, found in Famen Temple

Chapter 7
Gold Wares in the Song and Liao Dynasties

The Song Dynasty is traditionally divided into the Northern Song (960-1127) and Southern Song (1127-1279) periods. In both these periods, gold and silver craftsmanship flourished, especially with the expansion of the imperial and local official workshops. Historical records show that such workshops were found in almost every county and township. As trade flourished and crafts developed, new themes and decorative patterns were adopted, especially ones connected with the people's daily life and auspicious symbols.

Characteristic of this time was the springing up of family-owned gold shops. According to *Records of the Eastern Capital*, written in 1147 by Meng Yuanlao, gold and silver wares were widely used, not only by the imperial family and senior officials, but also by wealthy commoners, restaurants and brothels. The prosperity of trade and commerce in the capital Bianjing (now Kaifeng, Henan Province) is amply illustrated in the famous painting *Spring Festival on the River*, generally believed to be by the Northern Song imperial court painter Zhang Zeduan and now kept in the Palace Museum in Beijing.

■ Gold image of a boy, Southern Song Dynasty, unearthed at Jiaoguayuan Village, Quzhou, Zhejiang Province

The Story of Gold

Slim, Changeable and Antique in Form

The modeling and style of the decorative patterns of Song's gold ware were linked with the mild social mood at the time. On the other hand, they were affected by the trend of modeling after the antique and by literati's aesthetic taste. Such a trend led an aesthetic concept for the primitive, ingenious and tasteful, as that helped people to execute their critical self-examination and thoughts in depth. The most popular ideology at that time encouraged people to a kind of moral cultivation, for an internal balance and a strength in depth. The objects produced then featured a primitive shape and style, very often without even any decorative patterns, just like the tasteful Song Dynasty porcelain—simple without but intelligent within.

Gold objects produced in Song times were usually smaller and thinner than those manufactured in the Tang Dynasty, very often with a diameter of less than 20 cm for plates, bowls, etc. A gold earring found in a Northern Song tomb in Huxi Village, Pengze County, Jiangxi Province, is S-shaped and bears complicated patterns in relief. Some gold ornaments found in a Song Dynasty tomb on Mount

Mufu, Nanjing, Jiangsu Province, are exquisite and elegant. One of them, a small heart-shaped gold object, has an elegantly incised pair of phoenixes flying amidst roses and sunflowers, representing a lucky greeting. A heart-shaped gold sachet found in Xuancheng, Anhui Province, consists of two half-shells with twin dragon patterns on both the outer and inner surfaces, surrounded by blades of grass and a string of pearls. A gold dragon found in Yiwu, Zhejiang Province, 15.7 cm long and 1.8 cm wide, has a powerful posture, with high-raised head, long and curved tail and taut limbs. The fine craftsmanship in such a limited space is admirable.

A gold cup found in a Song Dynasty tomb in Xiuning County, Anhui Province, was hammed into a hexagonal shape. The bottom of the cup on the inside is decorated with three flower patterns and the upper and bottom rims have lightning patterns. The simple, plain and mild design and patterns represent the typical Song Dynasty style.

Modeling on antique designs and shapes is another feature of the gold ware of the Song Dynasty. From Huangyou reign period (1049-1054) on, the Song emperors were all keen artists and collectors of ancient bronze objects. This encouraged the production of imitations of bronze vessels in gold and silver. Craftsmen at that time even created a new "sandwich" technique, with one layer of metal sandwiched between two layers of gold.

■ Gold dragon, Song Dynasty, found in Yiwu, Zhejiang Province

The Story of Gold

Simple and Poetic Decorative Patterns

Many Song gold objects had very simple decorative patterns or even no decorations at all, whereas in the Tang Dynasty few gold wares were undecorated. A gold bowl in the shape of a lotus petal un-

■ Gold-plated octagonal silver plate, Song Dynasty, unearthed at Guxian Village

■ Gold-plated hairpins, Song Dynasty, found in Yongjia, Zhejiang Province

earthed at Pengzhou, Sichuan Province, has a diameter of 8.5 cm. This pentagonal bowl has no decorative patterns at all, probably to highlight the gleam of the gold. A gold cup found in Xiuning County, Anhui Province, with a hexagonal design has most of its surface undecorated. This pithy and poignant style is also reflected in the poems, and porcelain and lacquer wares of the Song Dynasty.

The themes of Song gold vessels fall mainly into three categories—poetic imagination, daily life and Buddhism.

A gold cup found in Gucun Village, Shaowu County, Fujian Province, is octagonal and completely plated with gold. The patterns on each of the eight outer surfaces match the content of the poems engraved on the inner surfaces. A gold-plated octagonal plate, also found in Shaowu, has decorative patterns of buildings and pavilions, engraved with fine lines and representing a kind of fairyland.

Other patterns are linked to ordinary people's daily life or represent auspicious plants or animals, including peonies, lotuses, litchis, pomegranates and peaches—which symbolize birth and happiness—and cranes, turtles and fish—symbols of longevity. A gold-plated plate has a decorative design of two lions playing with a ball. A silver box found in Quzhou, Zhejiang Province, has a six-gram gold figure of a boy inside. The naked boy is holding lotuses in his left hand and a ring in his right, thought to be good-luck symbols.

■ Flower-shaped gold cup, Song Dynasty, found in the tomb of Zhu Xiyan, Xiuning, Anhui Province

There were many gold items connected with Buddhism, such as statues of the Buddha, coffins and miniature pagodas, all bearing Buddhist symbols. A gold coffin found in a cellar in Fusheng Temple, Dengzhou, Henan Province, is decorated with an engraved scene depicting Nirvana. In it, the Buddha is lying on his side on a bed, with his head resting on his left arm, surrounded by six disciples. A gold-plated silver coffin found in the Asoka Pagoda in Haiqing Temple in Lianyungang, Jiangsu Province, has a similar engraved scene. In the center of the coffin lid is an image of the Buddha, with bare feet and surrounded with decorative patterns of *ruyi*, a wand which was a symbol of good luck in ancient China. At the foot and on both sides of the coffin are images of seated Boddhisattvas.

These objects are modeled on bronze ware patterns of the Shang and Zhou dynasties.

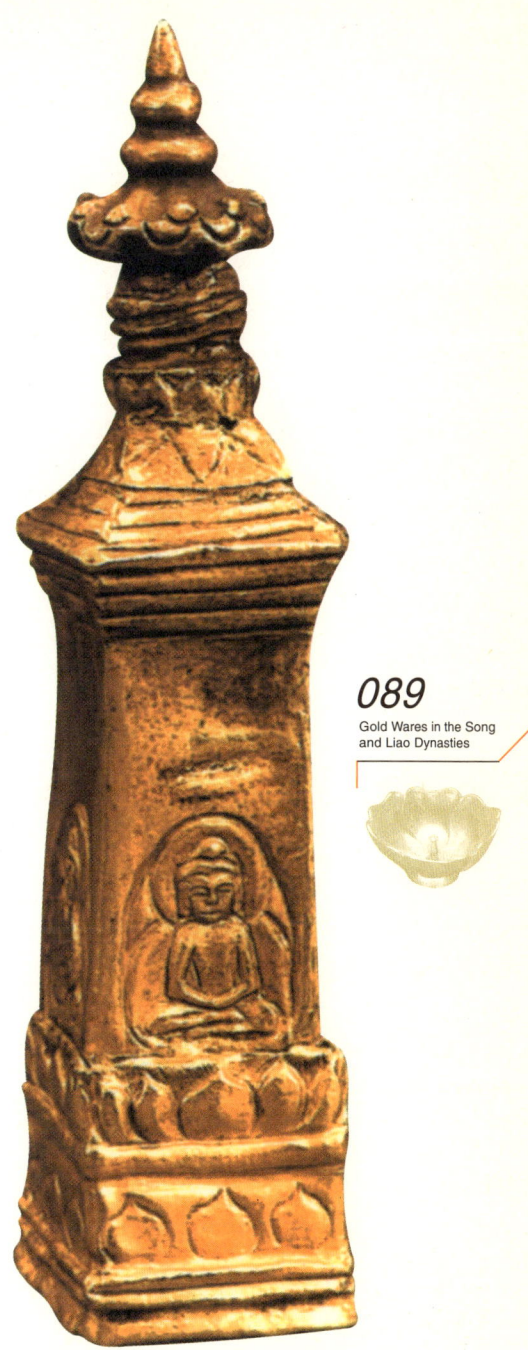

■ Gold miniature stupa, Song Dynasty, found in Chongsheng Temple, Dali, Yunnan Province

The Story of Gold

■ Gold Buddhist statue, Nanzhao Kingdom (Yunnan, 8-10th centuries), found in the Qianxun Pagoda at Chongsheng Temple, Dali, Yunnan Province

Gold for Decorative, Daily-life and Buddhist Use

Quite a number of gold wares in the Song Dynasty were ornaments and makeup boxes, indicating that, along with the dynasty's commercial prosperity and the wide purchase of silver and gold, women became important consumers. Such products remained a major gold category up until the Qing Dynasty.

Most of Song Dynasty ornaments so far discovered were from Yongjia County, Zhejiang Province. Most of them are gold-plated hairpins and hair clasps. The designs are simple, and U-shaped top parts are common. A gold hairpin found in Guayuan Village in the suburbs of Quzhou City in the province has patterns of clouds engraved at one end and curling leaves surrounded by small gold beads at the top. Two gold-plated makeup boxes were found in a Southern Song Dynasty tomb in Chayuan Mountains, Fuzhou, Fujian Province. One of them is in the shape of a hexagonal flower, with hammered patterns of double phoenixes on the cover, surrounded by decorative patterns of *ruyi* and flowers, and of curling leaves at the bottom. A gold-plated necklace found in the cellar of the Tianfeng Pagoda,

091
Gold Wares in the Song and Liao Dynasties

The Story of Gold

Ningbo, Zhejiang Province, is in the shape of a half-moon. It is decorated with images of a boy and peonies.

Song Dynasty gold ware also include bowls, plates, wine cups and sachets, all of which have been unearthed. A gold-plated heart-shaped sachet found in an ancient tomb in Huashizui, Anxian County, Anhui Province, is decorated with a pair of mandarin ducks on twin lotus flowers on one stalk, engraved in relief. A hexagonal gold plate found in an ancient tomb in Xiuning County, Anhui Province, has six groups of linked *ruyi* patterns in the center, two linked diamond patterns around them and two linked lightning patterns on the rim.

Among the products related to Buddhism unearthed are a gold coffin discovered in a cellar in the Jingzhi Temple in Dingzhou, Hebei Province, a gold statue of Buddha found in a cellar at the Tianfeng Pagoda, Ningbo, Zhejiang Province, and a gold-plated miniature stupa containing Buddhist relics discovered in the Huixing Pagoda, Rui'an, Zhejiang Province.

■ Gold-plated octagonal silver cup, Song Dynasty, unearthed at Guxian Village, Shaowu, Fujian Province

Creative Craftsmanship

Gold craftsmen in the Song Dynasty inherited the superb techniques of the Tang Dynasty, which featured such shaping methods as plate processing, casting, mold pressing and turning, and such processing means as cutting, polishing, welding, piecing, riveting, plating and engraving. Song craftsmen, however, introduced techniques of their own, such as sandwiching and relief sculpture for producing raised patterns. Fine craftsmanship can be seen in their products, such as in weather-consistent welding seams and steady machine turning.

Sandwiching was invented for modeling new objects on antiques, as bronze ware had thick walls, which forced Song craftsmen to sandwich a layer of metal between two layers of gold to reduce gold consumption.

Relief sculpture had been used in Tang Dynasty, but it was more popular in the Song, for raised patterns, especially for the purpose of making multiple layers. Pressing, hammering, semi-sculpture for raised patterns and intaglio were well-known techniques in the Song Dynasty.

093
Gold Wares in the Song and Liao Dynasties

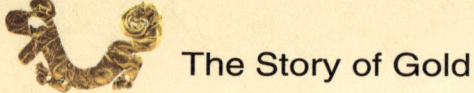

The Story of Gold

Gold Ware of the Liao Dynasty

Contemporary with the Southern Song Dynasty were the dynasties of Liao, Jin, Xixia and Dali, in the northern, western and southwestern areas of China. Gold objects were made in all these places, featuring unique ethnic styles.

■ Gold-plated silver *gui*, Song Dynasty, found in Liyang, Jiangsu Province

■ Gold coffin, Song Dynasty, unearthed at Jingzhi Temple, Dingzhou, Hebei Province

095

Gold Wares in the Song and Liao Dynasties

Gold ware found in the territory of the former Dynasty of Liao showed a gradual amalgamation of local cultural influences and the imperial standard patterns and shapes. Objects from the early period of Liao mainly included gold-plated silver ware, with Chinese images of peacocks and phoenixes, which, however, have the fierce-looking eyes of vultures. Later, gold wares focused on funeral attire and ornaments, with fewer ethnic features, and finally Liao gold ware became almost identical with those of the Song Dynasty's.

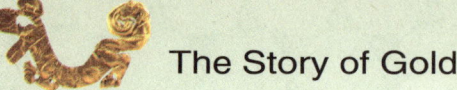

The Story of Gold

■ Heart-shaped gold sachet, Song Dynasty, found in Xuancheng, Anhui Province

A complete set of funeral clothes was found in a tomb of a princess and her husband in Jerim League, Inner Mongolia Autonomous Region. The hoard consists of a silver pillow with gold-plated flower patterns, a gold-plated silver crown, a pair of silver boots with gold-plated flower patterns, a gold mask and a net made of silver thread. This find is thought to represent the full funeral regalia of the Qidan nobility. The gold mask was molded onto the deceased's face. The pillow has patterns of fire, pearls, double phoenixes and clouds, all gold-plated. The gold-plated silver crown, surmounted by a figure kneeling in prayer, shows a high level of craftsmanship.

Also found in the former Liao area were some gold objects linked with Buddhism. An agate pot with a gold lid was found in the Heavenly Temple, Northern Pagoda, Chaoyang, Liaoning Province. The pot contains sarira (relics of the cremation of a Buddhist holy man) and five gold-plated pearls. Together with the pot was found a bird-shaped glass bottle with a smaller bottle inside it. It is believed to have been brought from Persia.

The Story of Gold

■ Gold-plated mirror case, Song Dynasty, excavated from Mount Chayuan, Fuzhou, Fujian Province

Two gold cups found in the tomb of Yelu Yu, Ar Horqin Banner, Inner Mongolia, are among the finest gold objects discovered in the former Liao area. One of the cups has hammered and engraved flower patterns on the inner surface, with the base rim and inner rim decorated with lotus petal patterns. The outer surface is decorated with patterns of four pairs of mandarin ducks surrounded by decorative patterns of flowers and cassia tree branches. The influence of the patterns common in the Tang and Song dynasties is obvious here.

One of the cups is in the shape of five flower petals. Its inner rim is engraved with curling grass patterns, and on the bottom of the inside there are mold-pressed twin-fishes splashing in water. The outer surface is engraved with lucky lotus petal patterns at the top, with five groups of curling grass and geese patterns engraved on the middle part. The lower part has lotus leaves, and there are wave patterns on the rim of the base. The cup shows Persian influence in modeling and Buddhist elements in the decorative patterns.

The Story of Gold

Golden-winged Bird from the Kingdom of Dali

During restoration of the triple-pagodas of the Chongsheng Temple, Dali, Yunnan Province, in 1976, 680 pieces of gold and silver objects were discovered. Among them were gold Buddhist statues, a gold-winged bird, gold miniature stupas and gold-plated boxes, of different styles, including those of the Tang and Song dynasties. The shapes of the gold Buddhist statues are reminiscent of those of the Tang and Song dynasties, together with local traits. A variety of crafts and processes were used during the manufacturing of these items, including casting, hammering, welding and engraving, which were practiced at that time in southwestern China.

The gold-winged bird, with a height of 18.5 cm and a weight of 125 g, is a gold-plated object with typical Dali characteristics. It is a holy object of Indian Buddhism and was thought to protect people from disasters. Standing on a sacred lotus pad, and inlaid with five crystal beads, the bird shows a high level of craftsmanship.

Chapter 8
Gold Jewelry from the Yuan and Ming Dynasties, Heyday of Veteran Craftsmen

In the Yuan Dynasty (1206-1368), the city of Suzhou, Jiangsu Province, emerged as the center of gold craftsmanship, with numerous workshops. Among Suzhou's leading gold craftsmen, the names of Zhu Bishan, Wen Xuan, Xie Junyu and Xie Junhe stand out.

Similar to the Song gold vessels, those of the Yuan period left large parts of the surface undecorated or adorned only with simple designs.

■ Gold crown with design of 12 dragons and nine phoenixes, Ming Dynasty, found in one of the Ming Tombs, Beijing

Rise of Handicraft Workshops

The Yuan rulers encouraged the extraction and processing of gold which, although forbidden to circulate, could be bought with paper currency. The mints would buy gold in exchange for paper currency, and then sell the gold as raw material to gold craftsmen.

Official handicraft workshops in Yuan Dynasty inherited the traditions of the Tang and Song dynasties. Wensiyuan (Imperial Bureau of Fine Crafts) owned dozens of workshops. The same as in other dynasties, the Yuan emperors often awarded subordinates with silver and gold, and local officials sent such tributes to the emperors. Gold

■ Gold ornament with design of intertwining branches, flowers and fruit, Yuan Dynasty, found in the tomb of Lü Shimeng, Wuxian County, Jiangsu Province

■ Jade *jue* (wine cup) with gold saucer, Ming Dynasty, found in one of the Ming Tombs, Beijing

plaques were awarded to officials for meritorious services or for identifying official ranks and posts. Such a gold plaque could weigh up to some 100 *liang*, engraved with lion, sun, moon images, and the title of the receiver's post and his obligations. The Tibetan Cultural Relics Administration keeps an official seal with "Seal of King Bailan" engraved on it in Phags-pa script. The king awarded the seal to Soinam Sangpo, who was made King of Bailan, a local Tibetan tribe.

In the later years of the dynasty, Yuan gold wares developed a tendency to become more resplendent and intricate, which had an impact on the styles of the later Ming Dynasty. Two gold ornaments found in the tomb of Lü Shimeng in Wuxian County, Jiangsu Province, are typical examples. Rectangular in shape, the ornaments have patterns of intertwined branches and fruit engraved in raised relief. Also found in the tomb was a gold decorative plate engraved with the scene of the story of King Wen of the Zhou Dynasty visiting the scholar Jiang Shang, who was fishing under a tree by a river. The vertical patterns were made in relief. Two holes are believed to be for a belt to pass through.

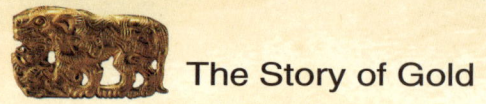

The Story of Gold

Unique Products

As many of the Yuan Dynasty's gold and silver objects had the manufacturer's and/or workshop's name engraved on them, some veteran craftsmen became well known. *Record after Retiring to the Countryside*, compiled by the early Ming scholar Tao Zongyi mentions the famed gold craftsmen at the time. "Among the leading gold and silver craftsmen in western Zhejiang Province are Zhu Bishan in Jiaxing, Xie Junping and Xie Junhe in Pingjiang, and Tang Junqing in Songjiang," he writes. It is a pity that no works by these people have been identified so far. Only some silver objects made by Zhu Bishan have been found, none of his gold works. However, over 30 gold objects made by Wen Xuan were found in 1959 in the tomb of Lü Shimeng

■ Gold hat ornament inlaid with gems, Ming Dynasty, unearthed at Zhonghua Gate, Nanjing, Jiangsu Province

■ Gold ring and rabbit-shaped ear pendant inlaid with a gem, Ming Dynasty, found in one of the Ming Tombs, Beijing

in Wuxian County, Jiangsu Province. Among them, a hammered gold plate with *ruyi* and cloud patterns has a unique design. In the center of the plate is a pattern of small flowers formed by the heads of four smaller *ruyi*. Other decorative patterns fill the rest of the space, executed by combining painting with engraving.

Gold hair ornaments have been excavated in Quhuisi Village, Lingqiu County, Shanxi Province, which are ranked among the best Yuan products. One of them has a figure of a flying Apasara and another has a figure of a dragonfly, all made with gold threads and displaying fine craftsmanship.

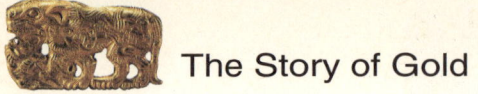

Luxury Jewelry

Most Ming Dynasty gold objects unearthed so far are items of jewelry. The biggest ones are those discovered in the Dingling Mausoleum, one of the 13 Ming emperors' tombs in Beijing's northern suburbs. It is the last resting place of the 13th Ming ruler, Emperor Shenzong (1573-1620) and his two wives. The 500-odd items of gold ware found in this tomb represent the acme of Ming

■ Laced gold ornament with *ruyi* design, Yuan Dynasty, found in Miyun County, Beijing

■ Jade bowl with gold cover and saucer, Ming Dynasty, found in one of the Ming Tombs, Beijing

handicrafts, and of them the emperor's gold dragon crown and the empress' phoenix crown are state-class treasures.

The dragon-patterned gold-threaded crown and the phoenix-patterned gold-threaded crown represent a typical mixture of all the gold processing crafts and skills inherited from the Song and Yuan dynasties.

The crown manufactured for Emperor Shenzong is the only gold imperial crown discovered so far in China. With a height of 24 cm, it is made up of layers of gold threads as fine as 0.2 mm in diameter. At the back, two dragons play with a pearl. The dragons have a total of 8,400 scales, woven in relief. Especially in the sphere of gold threading, this crown represents the highest gold craftsmanship of the Ming Dynasty.

The empress' phoenix crown features impressive inlaying of precious stone and pearls. It has nine dragons and as many phoenixes, together with more than 100 precious stones and 5,000-odd pearls.

Some gold dragon crowns, phoenix crowns, hairpins and hair clasps have been excavated from the tombs of princes, marquises and queens, such as those of Zhu

The Story of Gold

Houye, King of Yizhuang, Zhu Youbin, King of Yirui, and Zhu Yiyin, King of Yixuan, Jiangxi Province.

Gold crowns and ornaments have also been found in tombs whose occupants remain unidentified. A gold phoenix crown inlaid with precious stones was excavated in 1954 from the tomb of the tribal chieftain in Guizhou Province. It is padded with silver chips, decorated with patterns of gold dragons, phoenixes, lotuses and butterflies.

In 1977, a hat ornament inlaid with precious stones was found in a Ming Dynasty tomb outside Zhonghua Gate, Nanjing, Jiangsu Province. It has engraved entwined branch patterns with inlaid rubies, sapphires and turquoise, all surrounded by gold chips.

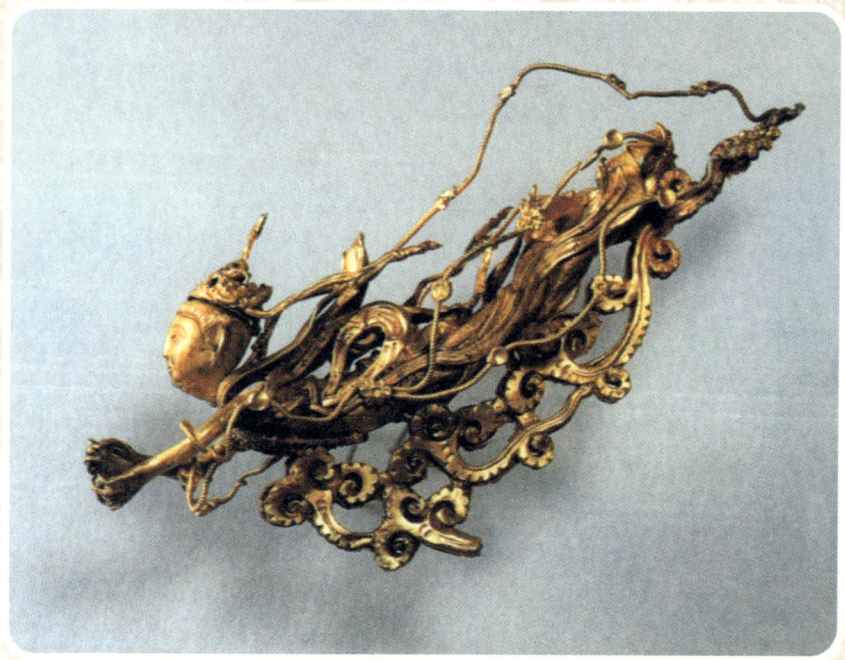

■ Gold headdress decorated with flying Apsaras, Yuan Dynasty, unearthed at Quhuisi Village, Lingqiu, Shanxi Province

■ Gold brooch in the shape of silver carp, Ming Dynasty, found in Zunyi, Guizhou Province

A large number of Ming gold earrings and finger rings have been unearthed, many inlaid with precious stones. Such objects influenced the gold craftsmanship of the following Qing Dynasty. A gold earring from the Dingling Mausoleum has a white jade figure of a rabbit preparing Chinese medicine, with its eyes made of rubies.

Gold earrings were also found in the family tombs of the king of Zhongshan, Xu Da, a famous general who helped finding the Ming Dynasty, in Bancang Village, outside Taiping Gate of Nanjing, Jiangsu Province. Two of them have a hooked upper part, covered with a plum-shaped hexagon inlaid with rubies and sapphires. The lower part is designed as a lotus pad, upon which stands a boy holding a basket in one hand and an unidentified object in the other. Several finger rings were also found in the tombs, with one having an oval cross section inlaid with turquoise. The ring was made using the hammering technique.

The Story of Gold

Vessels with Gold and Jade Inlay

Most Ming Dynasty ornaments were manufactured using the gold threading technique, together with the inlaying of precious stones and pearls. The Qing Dynasty inherited these traditions.

Among the gold artifacts found in the Dingling Mausoleum were household utensils, such as bowls, *jue* (a kind of wine cup), jars, medicine pots, makeup boxes and plates.

■ Gold dragonfly-shaped headdress, Yuan Dynasty, unearthed at Quhuisi Village, Lingqiu, Shanxi Province

■ Gold plate with *ruyi* design, Yuan Dynasty, found in the tomb of Lü Shimeng, Wuxian County, Jiangsu Province

   One of the objects is a thin jade bowl with a gold lid and gold saucer. The latter has cloud patterns engraved in relief, on which are two dragons playing with a pearl engraved in raised relief and a lotus-shaped knot inlaid with a ruby as the handle for lifting the lid. The saucer has a diameter of 20.3 cm and weighs at 325 g. It is decorated with dragon patterns, surrounded by rim patterns of auspicious clouds patterns. The pale jade forms a harmonious contrast to the shining gold.

   Likewise, the jade *jue* has a gold-plated saucer, which has a decorative pattern engraved in relief of a golden dragon flying out of the sea. The rim is decorated with a pattern of clouds and inlaid with 26 rubies and sapphires.

The Story of Gold

A gold *jue* with a gold saucer presents another feature. The inner surface of the plate has a decorative pattern of two dragons playing with a pearl. On the inner surface of the *jue* are similar patterns, and one of a cloud-shrouded cliff overhanging the sea on its outer surface. Both the *jue* and the saucer have inlaid rubies and sapphires.

Another gold-jade combination is a white jade pot with a round saucer. Found in the same tomb was a gold medicine pot, with the bottom engraved with the inscription, "Manufactured for imperial use in the Wanli reign period [1573-1620] of the Ming Dynasty, gold content 85 percent, weight 22.4 *liang*." Another inscription, on the belly of the pot indicates that it was exclusively used to decoct herbal medicine for the emperor. With the pot was an octagonal gold makeup box with dragon patterns engraved all over the surface.

One more gold-jade combination is a gold cicada resting on a jade leaf, in the collection of the Nanjing Museum.

■ Gold cicada and jade leaf, Ming Dynasty

Chapter 9
Flying Dragons and the Qing Dynasty

The number of gold objects handed down from the Qing Dynasty is enormous, including daily-life objects, ornaments and rare curios, often inlaid with precious stones. However, the most magnificent objects manufactured in Qing Dynasty were large vessels for ceremonial purposes.

The practice of combining gold with jade or pearls started in the Ming Dynasty and became common in Qing vessels.

The Qing rulers reserved certain decorative patterns to objects used by themselves alone. For instance, dragon and phoenix patterns became exclusive symbols of imperial power.

Although the Qing Dynasty had extensive contacts with the outside world, the gold objects handed down from that period show that modern scientific findings were only used, together with gold and precious stones, to manufacture rare curios for the entertainment of emperors and their concubines. The most typical of these are the armillary sphere and the celestial globe.

Most of Qing Dynasty's gold ware were handed down and reserved. And many of the household utensils, ornaments, ceremonial objects and Buddhist products are classic items.

■ *Ruyi*-shaped gold censer with carved patterns, Qing Dynasty

The Story of Gold

Imperial Ceremonial Objects

The ceremonial objects handed down from Qing Dynasty are all large, with an impressive or even record use of gold and pearls. To put this into perspective, the heaviest gold object from the Warring States Period is

a small gold drinking cup which was found in the tomb of Marquis Yi of Zeng in Hubei Province. It weighs 2,156 g, while a Western Han Dynasty gold animal weighs 9,000 g. The above-mentioned phoenix gold-jade crown of Ming Empress Xiaoqing weighs only 2,320 g. But, quite a number of Qing Dynasty vessels weighing more than 10,000 g have been preserved, including a four-armed, 90-cm-high seated Buddhist Goddess of Mercy weighing 31,800 g, and a gold 21.2-cm-high bell with a record diameter of 20.6 cm, weighing 24,500 g. A miniature gold stupa inlaid with turquoise and tourmaline and with a Tibetan-language inscription is 80 cm high and weighs 29,258.6 g. Another Qing miniature Buddhist stupa, 5.35 m high, contains 350,000 g of

■ Gold leaf issued by Emperor Daoguang confirming the authority of the 11th Dalai Lama, Qing Dynasty

The Story of Gold

gold. A set of chime bells made in the reign of Qing Emperor Kangxi (1662-1723) weighs 460,000 g.

The chime bells, used during grand imperial ceremonies, consist of 16 pieces. Each bell dangles from a figure of two intertwined dragons, and is engraved with patterns of auspicious clouds in relief on the upper part and twin dragons playing with a pearl in the middle.

A gold cup inlaid with precious stones was used at a special spring imperial ceremony. A wine drinking set has two handles shaped like *kui*, a dragon-like, one-legged monster in Chinese legend, with the heads each inlaid with a pearl. It is supported by a tripod with each of the three feet shaped like an elephant's head with a rolled up trunk. The outer rim has four engraved Chinese characters wishing stability and everlasting prosperity for the dynasty. At a ceremony held in the imperial palace at midnight before New Year's Day, the Qing emperor would fill the cup with a special wine called *tusu*, which means to dispel evil and awaken the soul, put the cup on a table and write the first auspicious characters for the new year, usually a wish for the state to be prosperous, the people to live in peace and the imperial power to be everlasting. The cup has engraved patterns of auspicious flowers and inlaid with rubies and sapphires.

The eight-treasure double-phoenix gold basin was carried before the Qing empress and the emperor's concubines. It has a wide rim with decorative relief-en-

117
Flying Dragons and
the Qing Dynasty

One of the gold chime bells, Qing Dynasty

The Story of Gold

■ Gourd-shaped gold flagon engraved with cloud and dragon patterns and inlaid with gems, Qing Dynasty

Gold seal awarded by Emperor Yongzheng to the seventh Dalai Lama, Qing Dynasty

graved patterns of such auspicious images as shells and magic fungus, surrounded with colorful ribbons. The patterns are all inlaid with red coral and turquoise. The inner bottom of the basin is decorated with such auspicious patterns as lotuses, phoenixes and curling leaves—all indicating prayers for a bumper harvest.

The Qing emperors inherited a suit of armor made of gold and silver and bearing intricate patterns. Manufactured by the imperial workshop, the suit, which took more than 40,000 man-days to make, is one of China's national treasures.

The Story of Gold

Imperial Treasures

Of the treasures of the Qing imperial court, the most precious is a celestial globe.

Manufactured during the period of Emperor Qianlong (1736-1796), it is the only gold celestial globe in the world that consists of three parts—the globe itself, the supporting frame and the base. The base's surface bears hammered gold patterns of sea waves. Above the base are nine dragons that support two rings holding the globe and symbolizing the equator and the horizon. The globe is engraved with meridians, and inlaid with pearls representing 300 constellations and 3,240 stars, with their names. The globe consists of two gold-hammered hemispheres welded together at the equator. At the top of the globe is a plate indicating the 12 two-hour periods which divided the day in ancient China. Below the globe is a compass.

Another masterpiece is a gold-plated armillary sphere, with moving rings representing the meridian, equator, white and yellow (lunar and earth) orbits, and such celestial bodies as the sun, moon, and earth with the meridians and continents, and their names. By moving the rings one can

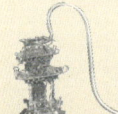

follow the revolutions of the sun, moon and stars, as well as interstellar interactions and various coordinates.

Qing craftsmen created a process linked with that for producing enamel objects, inheriting skills from the Yuan and Ming dynasties. They adapted the enamelware craftsmen's techniques of pot-burnt patterns and sectional fill-burn process to good effect. This process was especially popular in southern China's Guangzhou, where a gold hanging screen was manufactured, which is now in the collection of the Palace Museum in Beijing.

The screen has a frame made of red sandalwood, and a glass cover. It is painted with images of lofty mountains, rocks, bay trees in full blossom, billowing clouds and the moon. The rocks and ground are painted in vivid lines and the trees and flowers are pot-burnt with transparent enamel in blue, green and purple. The screen, a gift

■ A gold miniature stupa with Tibetan-language inscriptions, Qing Dynasty

The Story of Gold

for Emperor Qianlong from southern China's Governor-general Li Sirao, has a poem at the upper left-hand corner.

Among the treasures handed down from the Qing Dynasty are various categories of *ruyi*. On the 60th birthday of Emperor Qianlong, 60 gold *ruyi* were presented to him. Each of them has gold thread twisted into wires and then welded in certain patterns on the base. They are inlaid with turquoise indicating the Heavenly Stems and Earthly Branches of the traditional Chinese calendar.

Another ruyi has inscriptions reading "Boundless longevity" and "Presented on bended knee by your son Emperor Pu Yi." This must have been a present from the Qing Dynasty's last emperor to the Empress Dowager Cixi.

■ Gold *xi* (basin) decorated with flowers, "eight treasures" and two phoenixes, Qing Dynasty

Imperial Tableware

Tableware for imperial banquets or grand ceremonies all had unique designs, and were made of gold and jade.

Among various gold pots is one with engraved patterns of clouds and sets of standing dragons playing with a pearl (a pattern used exclusively by the imperial household), a total of 36 dragons. The pot has a pagoda-shaped cover of four stories, with each story engraved with twin dragons playing with a pearl.

Another gold pot has engraved lotus patterns, together with relief patterns of dragons and clouds. It is inlaid with ruby, sapphire and turquoise beads.

There are two eye-catching jade bowls. One, made of Yangzhi white jade produced in Hotan, the Xinjiang Uygur Autonomous Region, has decorative patterns of flowers, branches and leaves engraved on the outer surface. It is completely gold-plated and inlaid with 180 precious stones. The other is a high-stemmed white jade bowl with a cover and saucer made of pure gold, with engraved in relief patterns of lotuses. The bowl shows traces of western Asian culture in both the design and decorative patterns.

The Story of Gold

Imperial Buddhist Ceremonial Objects

The Qing emperors were all devout Buddhists, and spent lavishly on Buddhist ceremonial objects. A typical example of these is a four-armed seated Guanyin (Goddess of Mercy) made of pure gold. It is 90 cm high, and weighs 318 kg. The goddess' halo is inlaid with

■ Gold vase, Qing Dynasty

■ Laced gold ornament in the shape of a dragon carrying a pearl in its mouth, Qing Dynasty

colorful precious stones and has quotations from Buddhist scriptures engraved on the back.

Emperor Qianlong ordered the manufacturing of a gold miniature stupa to hold the fallen hair of his mother. A total of 3,440 *liang* of gold went into making it. The stupa has 13 stories, each engraved with quotations from Buddhist scriptures in Sanskrit. Inside the stupa are a gold Buddha and a rectangular trough holding the hair.

Displayed in the Jokhang Temple in Lhasa, the capital of the Tibet Autonomous Region, is a gold urn presented by Emperor Qianlong. It is still in use today for drawing lots to decide on the persons believed to be the reincarnations of the Dalai and Panchen lamas, the highest and second-highest religious figures in Tibet, respectively.

Gold Seals of the Qing Dynasty

The official seals of the Qing Dynasty emperors were made of various materials, including gold, wood, jade and stone. The seals of the empresses dowager and empresses were made of pure gold; those of the highest-ranking imperial concubines were made of 60 percent gold; those of imperial concubines, 50 percent gold; and those of princes and the imperial household's adopted sons, 40 percent gold. Official seals were classified as *yin* (seal, usually square), *guanfang* (government or army seal, usually rectangular), *qianji* (seal used by governmental organizations, usually rectangular) and *tuji* (mark). *Yin* were further classified as gold seals, gold-plated silver seals and copper seals.

In 1652, Qing Emperor Shunzhi invited the fifth Dalai Lama to visit Beijing, and in the following year formally conferred on him the title of Dalai Lama, and in April the next year granted him an official gold seal and an official gold certificate of appointment. The seal weighed 8.5 kg. The gold seal has a square face engraved with inscriptions in Chinese, Tibetan and Manchu languages, all with 26 characters.

Emperor Guangxu (reigned 1875-1908) gave his favorite concubine Zhenfei a gold seal weighing 6.8 kg. It has inscriptions engraved on it in both the Chinese and Manchu languages.

Qing official seals before the time of Emperor Qianlong often had inscriptions in Manchu only. In 1748, Qianlong ordered that official seal inscriptions be in both Chinese and Manchu.

Another important gold seal was that produced for Hong Xiuquan (1814-1864), leader of the Taiping Heavenly Kingdom, a rebel regime which challenged the Qing court. The seal is made of 100 *liang* of pure gold. After the collapse of the Taiping Heavenly Kingdom, the seal was stolen and melted down into 10 gold bars.

■ Dragon-shaped gold headgear inlaid with Japanese pearls, Qing Dynasty

The Story of Gold

Gold and China's National Ethics

As a precious metal, gold has always been sought after and treasured, manufactured into various shapes, and even enshrined and worshiped. Although down the ages gold was mostly the property of the emperors and the nobility, in the form of seals, crowns or masks, gold has long been an integral part of traditional Chinese culture.

This long acquaintance with gold has brought spiritual harmony to the Chinese people and resonance between the two. In the Warring States Period, a man in the State of Song offered a precious piece of jade to the official Dai Xi. Declining the offer, Dai Xi said, "I value honesty and uprightness most, while you value jade most. If I take your jade then we will both lose what we value most." This is the origin of the immortal Chinese admonition that one should take honesty and uprightness as things of the highest value.

One day, a man named Le Yangzi found a piece of gold. When he returned home, he told his wife of his good fortune. But, his wife was unmoved, and said, "I have been told that a noble-minded man will not drink stolen water."

■ Gold celestial globe inlaid with pearls, Qing Dynasty

129
Flying Dragons and the Qing Dynasty

The Story of Gold

Mortified, Le Yangzi returned the gold to where he had found it. This is the origin of a Chinese idiom warning us not to pocket any money we find by accident.

The Chinese insist that personality is the most valuable thing to maintain, and that friendship should be as pure as gold. There is an old story to this effect:

Guan Zhong and Bao Shuya were famous statesmen during the early Spring and Autumn Period, in the seven century BC. The two had been good friends ever since their childhood. Once, Guan Zhong shot an arrow at a snake that was about to bite Bao Shuya. It happened that a piece of gold was then found at the site. Each insisted that the other deserved to take the gold, and the affair ended with neither accepting it.

Later, the two cooperated in running a business. Guan Zhong often took more of the profit than was his due. However, Bao Shuya never considered this greedy because he knew that Guan was very poor and had to take care of his ailing mother. And Guan never explained his behavior due to fear of misunderstanding.

The friendship between Guan and Bao was marked by gold, and was as pure as gold. This was considered the hallmark of true friendship by later generations.

A common Chinese expression is "A hall filled with

■ White jade bowl with gold saucer and cover and Tibetan-language inscription, Qing Dynasty

131
Flying Dragons and the Qing Dynasty

The Story of Gold

■ Gold statue of four-armed Avalokitesvara (Guanyin or Goddess of Mercy) inlaid with pearls and gems, Qing Dynasty

gold and jade," which means being both wealthy and learned. In China, gold is often accompanied by jade, indicating purity on the one hand and gentleness on the other. Together, they are considered to make a perfect match. A "gold-and-jade marriage" is also a perfect match, as gold is a symbol of wealth, while jade is associated with good luck.

Chinese literature focuses on man, man's creation, cultivation and behavior, man's interaction with the universe, man's daily life and man's most treasured possession—life. The most memorable moments in Chinese history are often recalled as the "golden times."

In the Western Han Dynasty, wealth abounded throughout the land under Emperor Wen (reigned 202-157 BC). But his successor, Emperor Jing, declared, "Gold and pearls can neither serve as food when a person is hungry nor be worn to keep out the cold." He thereupon ordered that more attention be paid to agriculture and less to the making of precious things.

A common Chinese saying has it that true gold will shine no matter what the circumstances. This means that a man of integrity will be recognized and rewarded eventually.

The Story of Gold

Gold scroll with design of the moon and osmanthus flowers, Qing Dynasty

图书在版编目（CIP）数据

金子的历史 / 向中华著；周宗欣译. －北京：外文出版社，2006
（东西文丛）
ISBN 7-119-04521-0
I.金... II.①向... ②周... III.金（考古）－简介－中国－英文
IV.F416.32
中国版本图书馆 CIP 数据核字（2006）第 078116 号

作　　者：向中华
责任编辑：余冰清
英文翻译：周宗欣
英文审定：Paul White　李振国
封面及内文设计：天下智慧文化传播公司
制　　作：天下智慧文化传播公司
印刷监制：张国祥

金子的历史
*
© 外文出版社
外文出版社出版
（中国北京百万庄大街 24 号）
邮政编码　100037
北京外文印刷厂印刷
中国国际图书贸易总公司发行
（中国北京车公庄西路 35 号）
北京邮政信箱第 399 号　邮政编码　100044
2006 年(小 16 开)第 1 版
2006 年 12 月第 1 版　第 1 次印刷
（英）
ISBN 7-119-04521-0
7-E-3743P